The Bright Side of Depression

THE BRIGHT SIDE OF DEPRESSION

Jim Geddes

BROADMAN PRESS
Nashville, Tennessee

© Copyright 1985 • Broadman Press
All rights reserved

4250-16
ISBN: 0-8054-5016-5

Dewey Decimal Classification: 155.4
Subject Heading: DEPRESSION
Library of Congress Catalog Card Number: 85-17123

Printed in the United States of America

Library of Congress Cataloging-in-Publication Data

Geddes, Jim, 1935-
 The bright side of depression.

 1. Depression, Mental.   I. Title.
RC537.G43   1985   616.85'27   85-17123
ISBN 0-8054-5016-5 (soft)

Preface

This book is a Christian's attempt to present an overview of the authentic discoveries of modern scientific psychology as they relate to depression. The basic assumption is that these authentic discoveries of science form an amazing parallel with the biblical and Christian views.

The first task of the book is to define the nature and meaning of the *psychological depressions.* These are the characterological and situational depressions, and they make up 90 percent of all depressions. Characterological means a depression that points to the need for character growth and/or character change. Psychological depression should lead to character change, and this book describes the processes by which you can grow, develop, and mature your character beyond depression, especially if you:

—change your depressive thinking,
—change your depressive behavior, and
—change your emotional expression.

This book is not intended for the *medical depressions.* Ten percent of all depressions are medical and should receive medical treatment. They are biochemical, not characterological, and they do *not* respond *as well* to the challenge of new learning and personal reformation presented in this book for the psychological depressions.

The scientific and psychological viewpoint of the book is clearly *eclectic.* Very special thanks are due to:

Carrol Izard, for his outstanding work on the definition of depression;

Charles Costello, for his outstanding work on the adaptiveness of depression, and

Marcia Becker, for her penetrating criticisms and broad viewpoint.

The moral and spiritual foundation of the book is the New Testament, and the following concepts are employed or implied on almost every page:

- The New Testament's insistence on major personal responsibility for one's life, character, and conduct.
- The New Testament's confidence in the infinite creative wisdom of God, who made man's mind and who allows unpleasant moods and painful experiences to spur you to mature your character.
- The New Testament's confidence that major positive changes can occur in people, first, as the grace of God begins to work, and, second, as people respond to God's grace and take the responsibility to reconstruct their character.

Depression resolution often benefits from a blending of the scientific and the spiritual. This blending of the scientific and spiritual is the intention of this book. The scientific half of the blend is concerned with a careful definition of depression, the adaptiveness of depression, and strategies for breaking bad habits and learning new attitudes. The spiritual side emphasizes building a wholesome and workable conscience, as well as learning true beliefs and sound values.

Depression is an opportunity! As unpleasant and as horrible as it can sometimes be, depression is a unique opportunity that can lead to personal growth. When your life has come to a standstill because of your refusal to accept your losses, and when you have been refusing to adjust to your failures and disappointments, depression comes just at the right time to pressure you to smarten up and come to grips with the need for some major personal changes.

Depression is not a problem in itself. Depression is a necessary warning sign of the need to make changes in our character and life-situation. Depression is a natural prod to engage in serious self-analysis and personal problem solving. Depression is usually a constructive process, intended to slow us down for a better look at ourselves, with a view to making major changes in beliefs, values, and attitudes.

Depression should lead to character change:
—change in beliefs and attitudes
—changes in behavior and habits
—changes in life-style and priorities
—growth in personal and social skills.

After depression, you should be a better person with a stronger character.

Slow down, think straight, and make constructive changes in your life! That is the message of depression. So don't fight your depression; work it through successfully by making changes in your thinking, behavior, and emotional expression.

The outline of the guide is simple: First there are four chapters to acquaint you fully with depression and how it works, then two chapters on changing depressive thinking, then three chapters on changing depressive behavior, and finally two chapters on changing your pattern of emotional expression. Give yourself a fair chance to outgrow your depression by making a careful self-evaluation and changing what needs to be changed.

The Depression Attitude Test

What is your attitude toward depression? Mark the following statements as *true* or *false,* and then check your answers from the key* at the end of the test.

	T	F
1. Depression is a most unpleasant experience, but it is not a problem in itself. Depression is a necessary *warning sign* of the need to make personal changes in our character and life situation.	—	—
2. Depression is a *natural prod* to engage in serious self-analysis and personal problem solving.	—	—
3. Depression *should lead to character change:*		
• change in beliefs	—	—
• change in behavior and habits	—	—
• change in life-style	—	—
• growth in living skills	—	—
4. Depression is usually a *constructive process,* intended to slow us down for a better look at ourselves.	—	—
5. Depression is *usually not an illness.* Ninety percent of depressions are characterological and situational. Only 10 percent of depressions are biochemical and medical illnesses.	—	—

*Key: All of the above statements are *true!*

Contents

Part 1
Depression Should Lead to Character Change

1 What Is Depression and How Does It Work?........................ 15
2 Five Common Depressions and How to Outgrow Them...... 27
3 Depression as an Opportunity to Change and Grow............ 41
4 Depression ⟶ Character Change ⟶ Self Esteem 53

Part 2
Change Your Depressive Thinking

5 Live by True Beliefs and Sound Values................................. 63
6 Think and Reason Clearly 73

Part 3
Change Your Depressive Behavior

7 Increase Self-Control... 81
8 Update Your Life Goals and Revive Enthusiasm 89
9 Turn Anxiety into Motivation.. 97

Part 4
Change Your Pattern of Emotional Expression

10 Emotional Openness and Honesty 111
11 Assertiveness 123

Conclusions
Resolve Depression by Character Change

Conclusions 133

Part 1
Depression Should Lead to Character Change

Part 1

1
What Is Depression and How Does It Work?

Suzie and Sally are identical wives—at least you might think so. They are the same age, have the same marriage status, live in the same neighborhood, across the street from each other, and both have truly great love for their husbands. "He's the great love of my life," says Suzie. "My Sam is the right life partner for me," says Sally. Another way that Suzie and Sally are alike is that neither is depressed.

But then, as it can sometimes happen, both husbands die from illness. The wives experience, in equal and similar degree, the horrible heartbreak of the loss. Suzie is heartbroken; Sally is crushed and despairing. Each is temporarily staggering under the painful blow. Then Suzie slowly and surely gets her life back together and responds to the new life and future ahead of her, while Sally slips into a deep depression.

Sally's friends come to help her—"Come on, Sally, it's time to pick up the pieces, and it's time to look ahead." Sally instead gives the classic depressed responses, "If only I hadn't nagged Sam" (note the *guilt*). "If only I had gotten a second medical opinion for him" (more *guilt*). "If only that doctor had made a quicker diagnosis" (*anger* now). "I'm not sure if I'll be able to cope alone" (add *fear* to the list).

How do the two wives differ, so that one recovers from sorrow and anguish while the other slips into depression? Suzie's great sorrow slowly subsides as she begins to look at and accept the loss of her husband, but Sally's sorrow increases as she compounds it with guilt, anger, and fear.

So the age-old formula for depression:

1. Start with a heartbreaking loss or failure or disappointment or frustration, which results in sorrow and anguish.
2. Then add some other negative emotions to greatly complicate the whole problem, and which distract a person away from resolving it. Sally *added guilt*—"It's my fault!" and the guilt kept her focused on the loss, not on its resolution. She also *added fear*—"I don't think I can

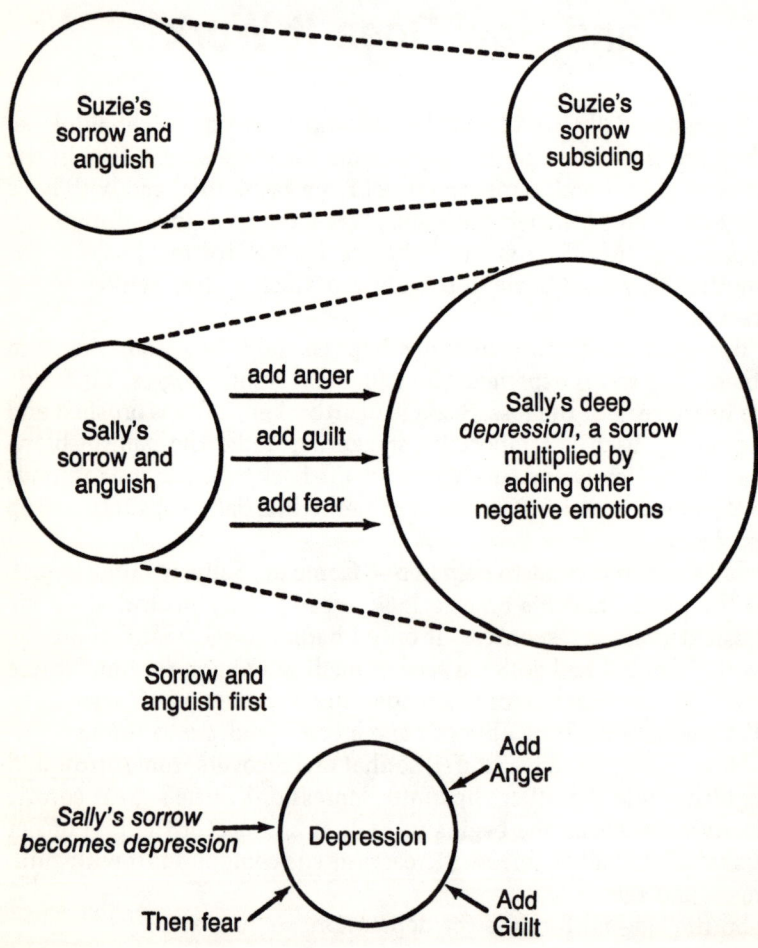

manage alone"—and this kept her preoccupied with possible negative consequences. She *added anger* ("It's the doctor's fault!"), and this also kept her thinking negatively and using her energy in frustration instead of resolution.

What emotions are you adding to your sorrow to turn sorrow into depression?

The Definition of Depression: Depression is sorrow and anguish that is combined with the other negative emotions of anger, fear, and guilt.

What are some possible combinations of the depressive emotions?

(1) *Sorrow and Anguish PLUS ANGER.* An employee is in *sorrow* and anguish because he was fired from his job. *Plus*—He is angry at himself for acting as he did while still on the job. If he had only the sorrow without the anger, he would not be depressed, only sorrowful.

(2) *Sorrow and Anguish PLUS GUILT.* A mother is in deep *sorrow* and anguish because her teenage son is so disrespectful and hateful toward her. But, in addition to her sorrow, she also feels deep pangs of *guilt* for the lavish attention and indulgence she gave him as an infant and preschooler, which formed the basis for his present arrogance and disdain.

(3) *Sorrow and Anguish PLUS FEAR.* Two lovers part. One of them is in intense *sorrow* over the loss, but is also *afraid* that future love relationships may all be short lived because his character does not have the basic trust needed for a permanent intimate relationship.

To resolve the depression, simply reverse the process, returning *from depression to sorrow* by resolving and removing the secondary partner-emotions guilt, anger, and fear.

Then the sorrow can be left to subside naturally by the passing of time.

Sally's friends helped her remove the guilt by changing her thinking. She then saw that her responsibility was to have made a reasonable effort to help Sam while he was alive, but she was not responsible for his death, just as she was not responsible for his life when he was alive—that was his responsibility. They reasoned with Sally until she straightened her thinking about the guilt.

Sally's anger took care of itself when the guilt was gone, as she

Sally's Emotional Combination

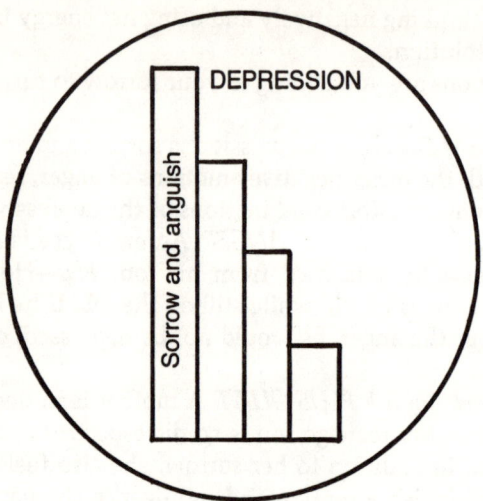

Resolving Depression

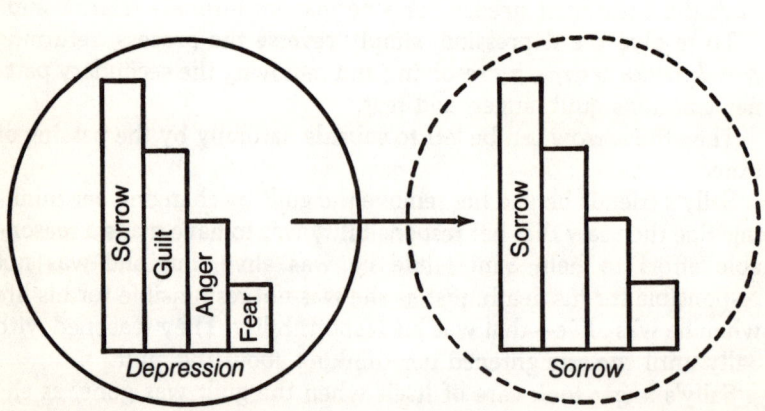

could no longer blame the doctor, just as she could no longer blame herself.

Sally's fear was more difficult to deal with—a fear of facing the future without Sam. Sally and her friends realized that this fear was rational because Sally was really afraid of failure in employment. They decided she would have to get more education to get the job she really wanted, so she took training as a medical receptionist.

The last line on Sally: she changed her thinking about her sense of responsibility and removed the guilt. She got more education to qualify for desirable employment and she removed the fear. Sally's depression was gone!

Sounds too simple? Actually, the analysis of most depressions is a simple process. It is the changes we have to make that are the difficult part of the process. Many depressed people know very well how and why they are depressed, but they stay depressed because they lack the willpower to break bad habits, or shyness prevents them from escaping loneliness, or lack of living skills produces further failures to break out of depression. Such necessary changes are easily understood, but very difficult to achieve, so the depression continues.

What If My Depression Is Biochemical?

Biochemical depression is an illness and can only be diagnosed and treated by physicians and psychiatrists. Biochemical depression is treated with medicines, shock treatments, and other medical means. Biochemical depression *cannot* be treated by reading this book!

Just as there is no psychological cure for medical depressions, even more so is there no medical cure for psychological or characterological depression. In psychological depression you must work it through yourself, with perhaps some counseling to assist you. The onus or responsibility in psychological depression is on the person himself to change his character, namely attitudes, habits, thinking, beliefs, or life-style. Ninety per cent of all depressions are psychological and characterological.

If you cannot locate a problem or cause that explains your depression as psychological, and if you cannot make headway against your depression, see your family physician for a psychiatric referral. You may have a biochemical depression caused by inheritance, stress, physical illness, or one or more of many other possible causes of biochemical depression.

The Range of Moods and Depressions

	Blues and Blahs (not depression)	Psychological Depressions	Biochemical Depressions
Severity	Mild	Moderate to Severe	Moderate to Severe
Type	Brief Emotional Reaction	Complex Emotional Reaction	Biochemical Reaction
Cause	Various minor frustrations and disappointments	Various life events and/or character deficits and/or false beliefs	Genetic tendency
Type of Help Required	None	Counseling or self-help	Medical-psychiatric treatment

Comparing Sorrow and Depression

Sorrow is an emotion which may occur by itself as anguish and sorrow over losses and failures, but sorrow may also occur as the dominant emotion in the depressive pattern. Note the following diagram which gives examples of *sorrow without depression* in the left-hand column, and then gives examples of *sorrow within depression* on the right. Only when anger, fear, and guilt are added to sorrow does depression occur.

Remember Suzie had intense sorrow-anguish without depression, while Sally's response is in the right-hand column because she had the sorrow-anguish, plus the other negative emotions.

Comparison of Sorrow and Depression

Examples of Sorrow	Examples of Depression
1. A man's wife dies and he is extremely distressed and sorrowful. But he is not angry, not fearful, and not guilt-ridden.	1. A man's wife dies and he is extremely distressed and *sorrowful,* but he is also *very angry* at himself for not having helped her enough during her illness. He also feels *guilt* about his failures as a husband. He becomes depressed.
2. A woman experiences sorrow and anguish over her failing marriage. But as sorrowful as she is, she is honestly facing her responsibility in the failing marriage. She is not depressed.	2. A woman experiences sorrow and anguish over her failing marriage, but blames herself (*guilt*) for the problems and is *afraid* to try to make it alone in the world. She becomes depressed.
3. A student fails an important exam and is in anguish that he will have to repeat the course. But he makes the necessary adjustments in order to pass next time. He is not depressed.	3. A student fails an examination and is in anguish that he will have to repeat the course. He is also very *angry* at himself for not studying, and he is *ashamed* to tell his parents and friends. He becomes depressed.

In each of these examples, sorrow alone is not depression, even if it involves intense grief and mourning. But the addition of other negative emotions creates the emotional pattern that is depression.

The Depression Emotions

From this comparison of sorrow and depression, it should be clear that depression is a *sorrow*-dominated combination of negative emotions. Let us briefly define sorrow and the other negative emotions:

1. *Sorrow* (remember the full term is sorrow-anguish): Sorrow is a response to (a) *losses*—such as loss of wife, friends, health, self-confi-

dence, employment, security, youthfulness, or (b) personal *failures or weaknesses*—such as bad habits, poor memory, false beliefs, wrong values, illusions.

2. *Anger*: In psychological depression anger often combines with sorrow. Anger is the complaint emotion, and *anger can be against self* in the form of a complaint about one's own weaknesses, or it can be *anger against others* in which case the complaint is against supposed injustice.

3. *Fear*: Fear is often one of the emotions in the depressive pattern and may be fear of suffering, fear of loneliness or rejection, or fear of failure.

4. *Guilt*: Guilt includes shame, shyness, disgust, and contempt, and is a frequent component of psychological depression.

A New Attitude Toward Depression

Depression, if it is psychological depression, is not a mistake or backward step. Depression is usually a forward step which results in significant personal changes, readjustments, and good decisions. It is the discomfort of depression that pushes us to accept the need for change. It is the slowing down of depression that gives the pause which results in a clearer look at ourselves. To consider depression as a basically positive or adaptive response is to have a new attitude toward depression. This depression self-help guide invites every reader to look for the good side of each depression. A new attitude toward depression itself is one important aspect of depression resolution.

When Is Self-Help Not Enough?

Is self-help enough for my psychological depression, or do I need professional help as well?

In most cases self-help is enough, but in others it is important to get professional help quickly. Here are the persons who may need professional help:

(a) Those who have no idea of the cause of their depression. Some

Depression Should Lead to Character Change

in this group will need only one or two sessions with a mental health professional, but this boost will help them get to the place where they can successfully handle their depression alone.

(b) Those with very weak willpower. These people mean well, but they simply will not discipline themselves enough to work through their depression on their own.

(c) Those who cannot read through this guide twice. It takes energy to work through a depression, and if energy level is too low, nothing much of value will come from self-help. So if you cannot read through this guide twice, you haven't got the energy needed for self-help.

(d) Those who have not had a good, recent medical checkup. They may have a depression-causing illness, in which case medical help, not self-help, is needed.

Most psychologically depressed persons do not require psychiatric hospitalization; or if they require it for rest and removal from the scene of their frustrations, they require it only briefly. What they usually do require is an opportunity to face their problems and think through the depression successfully. This book aims to guide their thinking through the stages of self-analysis, new thinking, and decision making that lead successfully through depression.

This guidebook is not simply a reading exercise, but a book for people who will make changes within themselves in their habits, reasoning, skills, attitudes, and values. A useful, helpful depression aims to accomplish just these kinds of inner changes: improved reasoning, new personal and social skills, better attitudes, sound values.

You are going to have a new and better life after depression because of the ways you have worked through the depression successfully and have made the changes that the depression requires. But change does not come easily, so be prepared for hard work to make the necessary changes. Don't just read this book but study the contents thoroughly by chewing, digesting, and reasoning through until you stop fighting your depression and start working with your depression to achieve the personal growth and change that the depression is pointing you toward. Your depression is not your real problem, but your depression is pointing to the real problem, namely, the changes you need to make in yourself and your life.

The Goals of This Guide

This guidebook offers self-help in several areas:

1. To provide an understanding of psychological depression in terms of the components of sorrow, anger, fear, and guilt, and to show how depression occurs when people do not respond effectively to *sorrow, anger, fear,* and *guilt.*

2. To offer a simple plan for depression self-analysis that leads to self-help.

3. To present the positive or adaptive view of depression which challenges the depressed person to look for the useful and life-serving purpose of each depression.

4. To offer techniques to turn depression into an opportunity for personal growth.

5. To discredit and disprove the faulty thinking and wrong values that cause many depressions.

6. To teach the personal and social skills—*emotional openness and honesty, assertiveness, stress control, self-control, self-esteem*—which help to lead out of depression.

The Depressive's Prayer

O Lord, I used to wonder if You had made a mistake in the way You created my mind. Otherwise, why would I be suffering the agony of this depression? Now I know the mistake is my mistake, because I took myself off in some wrong directions in the past, and depression is the consequence of my mistakes and wrong direction.

Receive my thanksgiving for Your creative wisdom in making my mind sensitive to error and sin. Now I see my depression as a painful, but necessary, step of character growth and change. Forgive me for blaming You for my depression. I take full responsibility for my depression.

Depression Should Lead to Character Change

Accept my determination to start to rebuild my character by finding true beliefs and sound values. Help me to break bad habits and build good habits. Help me to become that mature and strong person that I know I ought to be. Test me and try me as often as necessary until I measure up to the fullness of stature of a mature person. Amen.

2
Five Common Depressions and How to Outgrow Them

Depressions are often like the old Hollywood Western movies—the names of the heroes and villains change, but the plot remains the same. The dynamics of depression are often similar, and many depressions fit into five categories which are now presented here in five case studies. Probably you will see yourself in one or more of these cases, and you will then know the cause of your depression and what to do about it. Then the remaining chapters of the book will tackle your biggest problem, which is to learn how to do what you know you must do to outgrow your depression.

Study the Emotional Pattern of Your Depression

Before studying the first case, analyze the pattern of your emotions by looking at the diagram "Emotional Patterns of Depression." First, figure out the causes of your sorrow and anguish by identifying what it is you have lost out of your life. Second, identify which negative partner-emotions accompany your sorrow and anguish—namely, anger, fear, guilt, or more than one of these.

Study the Situation of Your Depression

Emotional analysis is not enough in itself—study your life-situation, too.
1. Are other persons significant in your depression?
2. Are there conflicts that perpetuate the depression?
3. Are there character weaknesses in you that prevent you from growing through the depression?

4. Are there critical moments in your life that are opportunities for you to succeed in your effort to change?

The following case studies will include these two approaches: (1) The emotion pattern analysis of depression, and (2) The situational analysis of depression. The bulk of the case study will focus on character changes that would resolve the depression, namely, changes in beliefs, attitudes, habits, and emotional expression.

Case 1—Alice and the Passive Life-style

Alice is a passive, young married woman whose childhood was dominated by a mother who criticized her and rarely gave her credit for any accomplishments. This left Alice with persisting doubts about her self-worth and self-confidence. Her uncertainty led to a passive life-style in which it was safer to do what she was told, be a follower, back down when confronted, and keep her opinions to herself. She married a man who also dominated her and criticized her homemaking and parenting skills. Finally, her own children are now dominating and criticizing her, too. She is very depressed as she has lost hope of ever improving her situation.

I said to her, "Alice, I would be depressed too if I were in your shoes. Tell me what it feels like." She told me of her sorrow and anguish over a marriage based on domination, not on partnership. She also expressed fear of loneliness as her children would be leaving home in a few years and Alice guessed her husband would leave too when he became bored with his domination of her. Then there was the anger Alice felt at herself for failing to change her character and become assertive.

Alice outgrew her depression when she enrolled in one course for assertive skills and another course for parenting skills. She studied, listened, reasoned, practiced, and slowly began to reconstruct her character and life-style until she became an exciting, assertive woman. Her husband and children fought back at first because they were used to the old mom who wore her passive chains quietly and who expected not even the crumbs of common courtesy and appreciation in return for all of her help. But soon they started to like the new

EMOTIONAL PATTERNS OF DEPRESSION

SORROW OVER LOSS OF:
1. personal identity
2. personal freedom
3. meaning and purpose
4. self-love, self-worth, self-respect
5. self-control, self-confidence
6. health—physical and emotional
7. hope
8. sense of security—at any level
9. goals
10. roles and status
11. employment
12. lover, spouse
13. son, daughter
14. parents
15. friends
16. structure and routine
17. usefulness
18. youth, appearance, beauty

ANGER:
1. anger at self—personal inferiorities —physical
2. anger at self—personal inferiorities intellectual
3. anger at self—personal inferiorities social
4. anger at self—personal inferiorities emotional
5. anger at self—personal inferiorities moral
6. anger at self—personal inferiorities bad habits
7. anger at others—interpersonal
8. anger at others—family
9. anger at others—social

DEPRESSION

FEAR OF:
1. death
2. loneliness
3. loss of love
4. loss of meaning
5. pain
6. failure

GUILT DUE TO:
1. failure in main responsibilities
2. living by wrong values, especially self-sacrifice
3. endangering or hurting others without cause
4. not standing up for one's own rights
5. bad habits
6. malingering, laziness, lack of self-control

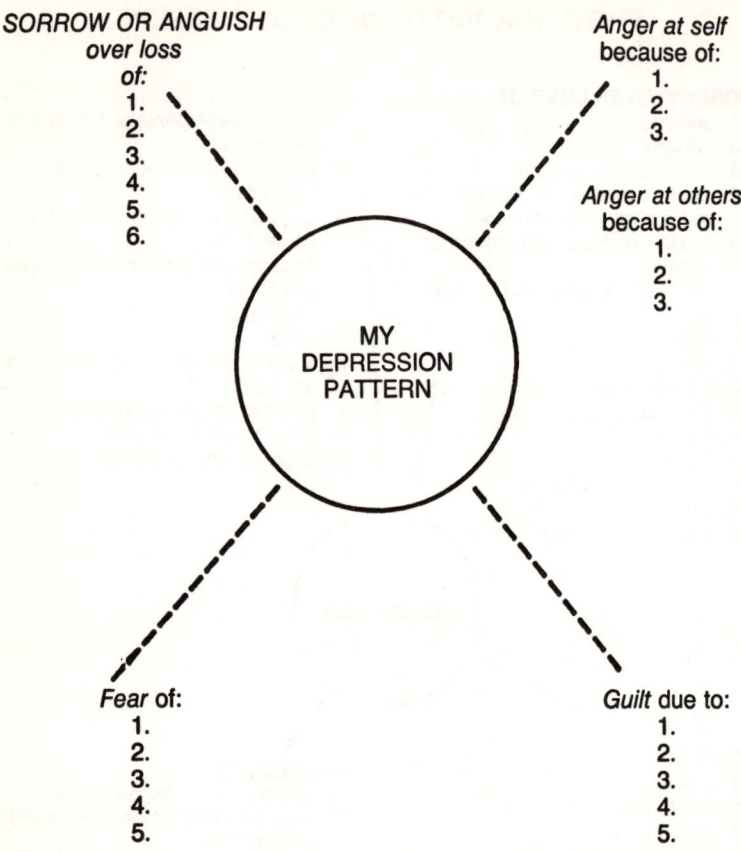

WHY am I depressed? What are the character weaknesses underlying the depression?

What are the stages of character growth leading out of my depression?

Depression Should Lead to Character Change

mom, mainly because she gave them back their self-respect by expecting them to do their full share of family chores. They also began to like her as she gently, but firmly, rejected all of their domination and criticism. Because they were treating her with respect, which she demanded, they came to respect her, too. Her depression was over.

Alice told me of several hurdles she had to leap as she worked on character change and outgrew her depression. First, she had to change some of her beliefs:

1. She came to believe that wives *must* be full partners in marriage.

2. She came to believe that her life could *only* be better if *she* changed. She wanted her husband and children to change, but this was the wrong focus. Rather than have her husband become less dominating, Alice had to become much more assertive.

Second, she had to change her behavior:

1. She found that good courses, offered in her community, were the key to her behavior change.

2. She recovered self-confidence by getting some success in the main areas of her life.

Third, one further change was necessary—a change in her pattern of emotional expression, by expressing anger and fear instead of bottling them up inside.

In summary, Alice found herself in a deep depression, and climbed out of the depression by means of character reconstruction, in which she changed some fundamental beliefs, some deep-rooted habits, and her emotional expressiveness. The route which led out of her depression is one that is being traveled by many other depressed persons; and it also leads them out of depression, provided they make the necessary character changes.

Case 2—Basil and Emotional Inhibition

How can so many bright, intelligent people get depressed? After all, aren't brains everything? The answer is no. Brains are not everything. Willpower is also important, and so are good habits and sound values. One person who found this out the hard way was Basil, the Brain, age forty-eight. This bright, middle-aged man was well educated and very successful in his own business. His problem was his inability to openly, regularly, and accurately express his true feelings. In his childhood his parents had always emphasized emotional control and dignified behavior. "Be courteous at all times, and be polite and proper in every situation," said his British father. Crying is frowned on because it is not manly, the family told him, and anger is uncivilized, fear is cowardly, and you never complain—you just keep a stiff upper lip.

As an adult, Basil remained true to his childhood. He was reserved, controlled, gentlemanly, fair, tolerant, impersonal, and lonely. How he really felt about life only Basil knew because his real feelings were hidden and suppressed.

But the man's wife and teenage children, and his acquaintances and employees, all misunderstood his dignity and self-control and, instead, considered him to be uncaring, a stuffed shirt, pompous, smug, and, worst of all, boring. They left him out of their lives because he was all logic and no fun. At times they guessed there was a warm heart behind the mask of emotional control, but if he wanted to keep his feelings hidden, that was up to him. So Basil, lonely and shy, full of emotions which no one knew, became depressed. His superior brain wrestled with the depression without success.

Look at the pattern of Basil's emotions. Notice how it is a repeat performance of many other depressions. First, there was *sorrow and anguish* over loss of close and meaningful relationships—and no wonder! Basil had been raised to suppress and overcontrol emotions, so his relationships were proper, distant, and formal, as though computer arranged. His marriage was a logical proper behavioral contract in which he performed according to rules—which is why his wife wanted out. To his children he was a financial adviser and a meal ticket, but not a person. Second, there was *anger at self*, as Basil realized it was his unemotional life-style that was destroying his relationships. He was failing to change though he knew he was the one who ought to change. Third, he was afraid of future loneliness and a meaningless life. Fourth, he was guilt-ridden over his failures as husband and parent.

The great day in Basil's life came when he began to work seriously at continuous, accurate expression of his emotions, and the results were amazing. First, he discovered that emotional expression reduced emotional pressure and eliminated his extreme outbursts. His son noticed that Dad was expressing emotions often, but Dad was no longer "exploding" twice a week. This control of the level of his emotional pressure at low and moderate levels gave him a natural and spontaneous control of emotions which people liked. They no longer needed to fear that Dad was about to explode.

Second, he discovered that he came to know his own emotions after expressing them. His wife said, "Basil, you are much easier to live with when we can share your feelings, but why do you feel guilty after expressing anger? You are expressing the anger—that's good. But express the guilt too and you'll then come to understand it." So Basil's emotional education raced forward as he came to know the interesting complexity of his own emotions.

Finally, he started to like people much more when he could be honest about his feelings for them—and the people, in turn, got closer to him as they found they could be emotional with him without his withdrawing in embarrassment. The final word on Basil came from his own lips. "My life is so much easier, and I can like myself better when my focus is on continuous, accurate expression of my emotions. I don't intend, ever again, to stagnate and suffocate in my own unexpressed emotions."

Case 3—Chuck and His Weak Conscience

Chuck, age forty, is happily married to the woman who is the great love of his life. Why then does he endanger his happy marriage? He recently attended a weekend business convention alone in another city and was involved in a brief but exciting affair with a much younger woman. He returned home hating himself and in sorrow and anguish, regretting his behavior because he knew such actions could endanger his marriage and family life. He was fearful that his wife and children might learn of the affair.

He hated himself even more after honest reflection as he realized he might very well seek out the young woman again when he attends the next business convention. As he faced the fact that he might seek her out again, he knew he could not trust his own conscience to control his behavior in his own long-term best interests. His fears multiplied as he sensed his self-control weakening and as he knew he was endangering the primary values of his life, namely, his marriage and his family. He became preoccupied with this weakness, his depression deepened, and he repeated over and over, *How can I be so stupid as to put my whole life on the line just for the sexual pleasure of a weekend? Am I going crazy to do such a thing?*

Many depressions, like this one, have a root cause in a weak conscience and inadequate self-control. Chuck couldn't control his sexual appetite and ran the risk of losing a wife who was easily the first value of his life. Others abuse alcohol and lose marriages, families, employment, health, fortunes, and self-respect. Others eat their way to ugliness and laziness—never because they really want to, but because they can't give up the immediate pleasure for a long-term gain. The list of excesses and addictions is endless—gambling, drugs, smoking, theft, marital unfaithfulness, overspending, overtalking, gossip, and so forth. All of these show a need to strengthen character by bolstering conscience and self-control, and failure to do so leads to depression. Is this lack of willpower or self-control the number one cause of depression in the modern world? Many experts think it is. Chuck knew his weak conscience and lack of willpower was the root cause of his depression, and his main task would be to find a way to make that conscience stronger.

So important is the problem of self-control that a full chapter is given later in this book to discuss the best means of increasing self-control. Chuck used a number of techniques and strategies discussed in that chapter. First, he confessed his problem to his wife and asked her to help him with the problem. She had suspected what was wrong but couldn't prove it, so she was at first hurt, then relieved, and finally pleased to try to help him. Second, he enlisted the help of a very skilled clergyman, who helped Chuck rethink his marriage commitment so that his commitment to the marriage increased. Third, he began to rethink the experience of the brief affair and to devalue the pleasure of the experience by comparing it with the much greater grand total of love and satisfaction of his marriage. Fourth, he made plans to reduce future temptations at weekend conventions. As he succeeded in these four steps, his conscience grew stronger and he outgrew his depression.

Case 4—Della the Martyr

This woman honestly and sincerely believed that martyrs make the best moms, but the truth is that martyrs make the worst moms. She deliberately set out on a course of self-sacrifice and always placed her children's needs first, considering her own rights and needs last, if at all. This acceptance of martyrdom or self-sacrifice was her false value, and because of it she could never explain the worsening annual mood cycle of her spring and fall depressions, during which her family's demands were greatest and her satisfactions least. Neither could she understand why her children took her for granted and did not show appreciation for her self-sacrifice. But why should they show appreciation? After all, she had convinced them that she should sacrifice herself to them. So they expected her to get on with the sacrifice, and hurry up about it, too. She worked hard on their behalf, and they expected it. If she ever did something nice for herself, they told her she was selfish!

Her false thinking was her belief that if she denied herself for them now, then someday they would appreciate her and return all the kindness. But the fact was that as they received so much from her without even giving payment of common courtesy and a show of appreciation, they came to despise and hate her, not to appreciate her. They started to demand more and more, which she tried to give and couldn't. Then, when she finally had to deny such impossible demands, they pressured, threatened, and accused her of not caring for them.

She had good reason to be depressed. In her desire to be the best possible mother, she had created monsters by being a slave and a doormat upon which her children wiped their feet.

The pattern of her emotions emphasized sorrow and anguish for the loss of her children's love and respect. They despised her; she knew it; and it broke her heart. She was also angry, first at herself for creating this parent-child problem and, second, at the children for their discourtesy and unkindness.

Della finally realized that her wrong values and false thinking were the real problem. It was not up to the children to change; she was the one who needed to change. She was a mother who wrongly believed in martyr parenting. She wrongly believed self-sacrifice pays off in the long run. But the facts were all against her and she was doomed to continuing disappointment unless she changed her thinking and actions as a parent. In her desperation she started to read books on parenting, enrolled in a course on parenting skills, made important changes in herself, and worked through the depression successfully. The children tried to keep their martyr mom, but the new mom persisted and finally earned their acceptance and respect. How? Mainly by Della's giving up the idea of self-sacrifice and insisting firmly that helping in the family must work both ways.

Can depressions sometimes occur to a person who is too nice, too helpful, overly considerate, willing, and kind? Della is the answer. The day came when she refused to do more than her fair share, went on strike if they were not appreciative, and always demanded her full share of free time and surplus family income. The depression then lifted.

Case 5—Ed Meets Three Misfortunes

Depressions can come because there is just too much misfortune at once. Ed lost his left hand in an industrial accident, and he suffered anguish and sorrow more deeply than he realized. Only one month later he was fired from a most satisfying job. Then, three weeks later, while he was still unemployed, Ed's house and personal effects were destroyed by fire. He might have had any other string of discomforts in rapid succession, but these were enough to confuse him, cause him distress and anguish, make him question whether God was against him, and raise serious doubts about his own sense of purpose, his goals, and his capability. In trying to resolve so many problems at once, he lost his self-confidence and became depressed.

Depression Should Lead to Character Change

The emotional pattern in such cases is the same—anguish and sorrow compounded by anger and fear. The character weaknesses are not so apparent and not so critical, but it was clear that Ed had to rebuild his self-confidence by exercising patience and good judgment. The first task was to set new realistic goals related to employment and his lost hand. He took training in a new line of work, learned to use his artificial hand effectively, and finally regained employment. His depression lifted as soon as he had enough time to think through his misfortunes and accept the serious losses, make the necessary adjustments, and begin to look ahead with hope toward the balance of his life.

Depressions almost always come from the need for character change, and the correct character change resolves the depression. But Ed's need, and the need of some other depressives, was for character growth. When life hit him with a series of misfortunes that were greater than he had ever faced before, character growth was an important step in facing this bigger challenge. Ed tested himself and knew he had to strengthen his basic principles of character, especially acceptance of reality, acceptance of self, and acceptance of reason as his rule for life. The depression was really a test to commit himself more deeply to his own pursuit of happiness and integrity. Ed outgrew his depression by this gradual growth of character.

Many adolescents and young adults have depressions caused by a series of misfortunes that became too heavy to bear at once. Character growth must be the response to such a depression. It might be called "growing up in a hurry" or "facing harsh reality," but character growth is the nature of the change.

Other Depression Crises

There are many other less common depressive profiles, including:

1. *The Crisis of Aging.*—Some elderly persons are unable to accept the fact of aging, just as certain younger adults are unable to respond to the challenges that are unique to each decade of the life span. Depression often occurs when we do not accept our age, and we are forever

wishing we were younger, or we wish our youth (or middle age) had been different than it was.

The myth of the twilight years is a view that elderly persons cannot be active and happy because their minds are weak and worn out. This myth, when believed by an elderly person, is a regular cause of depression. The fact though is that elderly persons are wiser, know more, and are well able to be productive and creative throughout the second half of life, except where ill health prevents it.

2. *The Crisis of Ill Health.*—Depression often follows ill health as a direct effect. Many illnesses are known to lead frequently to depressions. Even minor illnesses and minor handicaps can lead to depression. It is important to monitor ourselves in all illnesses from flu to pneumonia, to be on guard for the ill health that can lead to depression.

3. *The Crisis of Immaturity.*—Immaturity means we are growing in self-control and good judgment at a rate slower than average. Because our self-control is weaker and because our thinking is less logical, due to immaturity, we are more depression prone. We should be on guard to get advice and counsel on the major decisions we have to make.

Completing Your Depression Self-Analysis

From the foregoing case studies you should be thinking that while depressions are all different, they are also very much the same.

Let's list what depressions have in common:

1. There is gloom and dissatisfaction with life as we find it now, especially in important relationships.

2. There is a natural slowing down, a temporary paralysis and recoiling from loss.

3. There is often a hatred of one or more parts of self and a recognition of the need to change these parts.

4. There is sorrow-anguish, the major depressive emotion, over one or more losses or failures or disappointments; and there may be varying amounts of fear, anger, and guilt, which are the other depressive emotions.

Depression Should Lead to Character Change

5. *The causes of depression are many*, including major losses, setbacks, recurring disappointments, perceived inferiorities, injustices, dangers, weaknesses, false values, wrong thinking, passivity, lack of self-control, feelings of helplessness and inadequacy, inhibition, ill health, aging, immaturity, lack of social skills, and so forth. This is a big list of possible causes, and out of the list, your own causes of your depression must be identified.

6. Depression occurs only when a person is unready or unwilling to make necessary changes to bring one's life back on the track of actively pursuing one's fullest happiness in a balanced and practical way.

7. The final point in self-analysis, which introduces the next chapter, is that there is an adaptive or useful purpose to depression, namely, depression gets me to focus on the areas of my life that I want to improve.

You Probably Don't Need a Miracle!

Is depression something to pray about? Of course it is; but God, who is sovereign over every thought, action, and feeling, will not go against His plan and purpose for the depressed person. He has a plan for you to be a better person, and He may use the depression as part of His plan.

God listens to prayer, and He answers. So be careful to word your prayer wisely. Don't ask him to take away the depression yet. Ask Him to help you use your own eyes to see what is wrong in your life. Ask Him to help you use your mind to struggle to become a better person, a mature person. Ask Him to help you to use your own feet to get going where you know you need to go. Seek His guidance in changing directions, priorities, attitudes, and habits.

Do not pray "Lord, take this depression away." Instead, pray, "Lord, help me to work through my depression successfully. Help me to outgrow my depression. Help me to change what I need to change in my life, so that I can mature beyond depression."

Solomon's Wisdom Led to Depression

A little knowledge is a dangerous thing. King Solomon of ancient Israel had knowledge about zoology, botany, and governmental administration, but he didn't know himself. Now what is more important—knowledge of zoology or knowledge of self? Solomon became very depressed as a way of discovering his own lack of self-knowledge. Finally, in humility over how ignorant he had been of self, he was able to rebuild his life.

Listen to his own account of the story:

> I built myself houses . . . vineyards; . . . gardens. . . . I bought slaves, male and female. . . . I had possessions, more cattle and flocks than any of my precedessors in Jerusalem; I amassed silver and gold. . . . I was great, greater than all of my predecessors in Jerusalem; and my wisdom stood me in good stead. Whatever my eyes coveted, I refused them nothing, nor did I deny myself any pleasure. . . . Then I turned and reviewed all my handiwork, all my labour and toil, and I saw that everything was emptiness and chasing the wind, of no profit under the sun.
>
> So I came to hate life, since everything that was done here under the sun was a trouble to me. . . . So I came to hate all my labour and toil. . . . Then I turned and gave myself up to despair.
>
> There is nothing better for a man to do than to eat and drink and enjoy himself in return for his labours. And yet I saw that this comes from the hand of God. For without him who can enjoy his food? . . . God gives wisdom and knowledge and joy to the man who pleases him (Eccl. 2:4-11,17-18,20,24-26).

Solomon, before his depression, was a conceited and ignorant man. After his depression Solomon was a much better person—wiser about self, wiser about life, wiser about God's ways. So it is with every psychological depression—it should leave you a better person.

3
Depression as an Opportunity to Change and Grow

Depression as an Adaptive Response

There is a bright side to every depression—the positive side of depression. Every depressed person knows the negative side, but the key to depression self-help is in understanding the positive or adaptive side of depression.

Adaptive means having a useful purpose that adds to the quality of life. Adaptive responses are useful—on the right track—having a positive value. Adaptive responses are always life-serving, life-preserving, and life-enhancing. Adaptive responses are never a mistake; they are never illnesses, even though they are often unpleasant at the time. This may sound like a contradiction, but adaptive responses are sometimes unpleasant. A good example is vomiting, which is an unpleasant experience in itself, but which serves the life-preserving function of emptying the stomach of contents that are unacceptable to it. How awful it feels to vomit, but how good it feels afterward. This is a paradox of many adaptive responses: namely, they are unpleasant but they do lead to an improvement in life. Other unpleasant adaptive responses are coughing, sneezing, toothaches, hiccups, and crying—all unpleasant, but all useful and life-serving.

The Adaptive Functions of Depression

What are the adaptive functions of depression? How is depression a positive process? How is it necessary for survival? How does it lead to a better life? The adaptive functions of depression are as follows:

1. *A slowing down function.*—Depression slows us down so we can

think more rationally. Depression slows us down to have more time for major decisions. Careful thinking takes lots of time; and careful analysis of each alternative will lead to the best solution. Depression buys us the time to slow down and think straight.

2. *A focusing function.*—Remember the case of the dominated wife who became depressed and then had no interest in anything except to figure out how to be an equal partner in relationships? A proper function of depression is to cause us to focus on one particular aspect of our life until we improve it. Our interest in other areas of our life grows weaker and weaker, and we narrow our attention to the crisis at hand.

3. *A motivating function.*—The motivation of depression is a specific motivation to focus on changes that have to be made in ourselves and also in our primary relationships. Depression motivates us to face problems, not to run away from them.

4. *A cushioning function.*—Depression insulates us temporarily from intense psychological pain. This is the numb feeling of depression. It cushions us to withstand the impact of major losses by giving us more time to accept them. A good example is the woman whose husband dies suddenly, and she says, "I am still in the shock of his death, and I may not feel the full loss until after the funeral when the visitors have gone home."

5. *A protecting function.*—Another adaptive function of depression is to protect us from making any decisions until we have more time to carefully analyze the present crisis. This protection comes as a type of temporary mental paralysis and postponement of decisions. This paralysis remains with us until we have had an opportunity to study a major loss from all angles.

Depression Always Aims At a Better Life!

Depression is a necessary and positive response. Depression points us to critical areas of our life that are in need of repair and improvement; it insists that we use our mental energy and ability to find solutions and put these solutions into adaptive changes that will

Depression Should Lead to Character Change

satisfy us. The final goal and objective of every depression is one or more of the following improvements:

1. *Character Growth*
   —more self-control
   —better understanding of reality
   —better acceptance of reality
   —straighter thinking
   —new personal skills
   —new social skills
   —continuous, accurate emotional expressiveness
2. *Character Change*
   —greater self-control
   —rejection of some false reality
   —breaking of bad habits
   —improved relationships
   —better employment
   —better health

Don't Fight Your Depression!—Work It Through

Why is the adaptive view the key to understanding depression? The adaptive view is the key because it informs you that depression is not your problem. The enemy is the problems you have not resolved—perhaps some bad habits, or some self-defeating attitudes, or some wrong values. Maybe the problem is your lack of self-confidence, shyness, emotional inhibition, or undue pessimism or optimism; but depression is not the problem. Depression is your own mind's final attempt to have you face the problem honestly and work the problem through to a resolution. Your worst mistake would be to miss the point and see the depression as the problem. Your wisest move would be to cooperate with your depression as it leads you to extremely serious self-analysis with a view to consider making major changes in your life. So work *with* your depression, not *against* it. It is giving you a profound message that you may have to overhaul and rethink and reorganize one or more particular aspects of your life.

Significant personal changes and readjustments are the healthy consequences of working cooperatively with your depression.

Depression as a Prelude to Personal Growth

Depressions are opportunities, but they have to be worked at or the opportunity is lost. Depression means that some things in you have to change—maybe you need a new skill or a new attitude or a new habit—but if you work to acquire the skill that your depression is focusing on, then your life is going to move forward. This is why successful depressions are preludes to personal growth. First, you recognize the requirements for growth and inner change. Then you work, struggle, and agonize, if need be, until you have met these requirements. Then, with the barriers and obstacles removed, you can give your life the sparkle and luster that you have earned by working through the depression successfully. Many spurts of personal growth and maturity have resulted from successful depressions.

The Depressive Emotions as Adaptive

Depression is an adaptive response, but each of the negative emotions of depression is also adaptive or life-serving. These negative emotions, because they are adaptive, must not be considered as the problem. In fact, each of them—sorrow, anger, fear, guilt—makes its own special contribution toward the solution of the problem, that is, provided you look to find the adaptive aspect of each negative emotion. To help you do this, the special adaptive functions of the negative emotions are identified as follows:

1. *Sorrow and Anguish*

This is the major depressive emotion. It usually includes feelings of sadness, unhappiness, distress, misery, discouragement, dejection, gloom, and despair. Its function is the slowing down function, for more accurate perceptions, and as a prelude to directional change and adjustment. Another function of sorrow is the focusing function in which we focus on our major losses, which might include some of the following:

Depression Should Lead to Character Change

- loss of personal freedom
- loss of meaning and purpose
- loss of self-worth
- loss of health—physical or emotional
- loss of sense of security—including marital, occupational, financial, etc.
- loss of employment
- loss of spouse, family, or friends

The sorrow emotion causes us to dwell on our losses—but in constructive ways, namely: to minimize our losses, to prevent recurrence of losses, and to see in what ways, if any, our life-style is responsible for the losses.

One writer, E. S. Paykel, has suggested seven types of events which most commonly precipitate sorrow (E. S. Paykel, 1969):

- marital separation
- death of an immediate family member
- departure of a family member from home
- increase in arguments with spouse
- start of new type of work
- serious illness of a family member
- serious personal illness

In these events, sorrow is precipitated to determine how much I am responsible, what significant change will result from the event, and what I should do about it. Also, the purpose of sorrow is to attract the attention of others to our situation and needs.

2. *Anger*

This is the complaint emotion, and it includes feelings of anger, fury, rage, hatred, resentment, and irritation. Anger's functions are: the *pointing* function, in which we aim our anger in directions where we want a better deal, and the *motivating* functions, where we are motivated to search for a means of resolving a problem.

Inner-directed anger provides the motivation for self-growth. We hate a part of self and then try to change it, such as:

- physical inferiorities—acne, obesity, poor vision;
- *intellectual* inferiorities—poor memory, weak reasoning skills, lack of education, poor concentration;

- *social* inferiorities—shyness, passivity, poor conversational skills, bad habits;
- *emotional* inferiorities—inhibited, aggressive, impersonal;
- *moral* inferiorities—*lack* of willpower, lack of values, false values.

Outer-directed anger provides the motivation for a search for justice. It is evidence of frustration in dealing with others, and it motivates a search to answer the question "How can I get a better deal for myself?" The concern about injustice may be on several levels:

- *interpersonal injustice*—unfairness by a neighbor, fellow employee, or friend.
- *family injustice*—unfairness and unkindness by a spouse, son, daughter, parents, in-laws, or other family members.
- *social injustice*—unfairness by government or other public and private institutions and organizations.

The adaptiveness of anger—of both inner-directed and outer-directed anger—is in its expression. Anger, when expressed, initiates contact with those we suppose to be the source of injustice and stimulates dialogue with them. It musters energy needed for a persistent searching for an answer that will end the injustice. Anger, when unexpressed, keeps the mind searching for possible solutions until there are so many that it bogs down untested possibilities. Only by expressing anger can we get the feedback information to test any possibility for its value. *Unexpressed* anger increases depression. A major cause of depression in adults is suppressed anger, which often stems from childhood training. One common goal of many depressions is the unbottling and release of anger.

3. *Fear*

Fear is often present in depression but is never dominant. Its function is to give danger signals to spur us to action. Fear includes feelings of panic, terror, apprehension, and dread. Fear works in stages, and in its first stage it gives a burst of mental energy to assess the danger and plan how to deal with it. Then fear gives a burst of muscle energy to execute the plan. Adaptive fear gets us to think and then to act.

The basic fears are all adaptive or life-preserving, and they include: fear of pain (including illness); fear of loss of love and friendship

Depression Should Lead to Character Change

(including marital and family); fear of loneliness (elderly persons do not need so many relationships of intense involvement, but they do fear being alone and outside of group activities; fear of loss of meaning and purpose; fear of failure (marital, social, financial); and fear of death.

Fear is related to sorrow, the basic emotion of depression, in that sorrow motivates us to serious self-analysis of past losses and failures, while fear motivates us to predict and avoid future losses and failures.

Irrational fears are present when our mental assessment of danger is inaccurate, and the danger is different than we see it to be. We can only tell if a fear is irrational in two ways: (1) someone persuades us that we have reasoned it out wrongly, or, (2) we assess it further and correct our assessment.

The fundamental role of reason and assessment means, in common daily occurrences, that we are always using reason to revise our assessments and outlook, but always in one direction: from irrational toward what we currently believe is rational. This again is the adaptive side of fear; namely, it spurs us to the use of reason and good judgment.

Are some people too fearful? Yes, there are a small number of people who are very sensitive to pain and other stresses, and these people are very fearful. However, they do not have more than their share of *depressions*. They do have more than their share of *anxiety*.

4. *The Guilt Pattern*

This combination commonly includes shame, disgust, and contempt, and its function is to focus on ideals and workable personal values. The adaptive aspect of guilt is its aim at not just the minimum required for survival, but rather *the maximum that is possible for each person*.

The shame emotion, which includes feelings of humiliation, shyness, and embarrassment, constantly compares us with our fellow humans and uses our pride to get us to compete to be better than others in all of the main lines of human endeavor. While this emotion can sometimes push us to the point of overwork, it is obviously adaptive in trying to secure as many benefits of life as possible. Without adequate shame, we settle for mediocrity.

The disgust emotion gives us an aversion and distaste for any values we think to be inferior to our own and keeps us conscious of the lower limit of our own moral standards. It is adaptive in this role of keeping clear the lines between acceptable and unacceptable behavior.

The contempt emotion, which includes the feelings of scorn, sneering, disdain, haughtiness, and derision, causes us to reject those persons of lower standards and acts as a negative selecting device to use to break off and terminate relationships with those of unacceptable value systems. Inadequate contempt makes us indiscriminate in our choice of partners and friends.

This shame/disgust/contempt pattern (*guilt*) works in a number of useful ways. First, it builds willpower and resistance to temptation by increasing our commitment to what we believe in. This increased commitment is essential in ridding ourselves of strong, but undesirable, habits which we want to break. As we increase our commitment to our beliefs, we are rebuilding and restructuring our conscience, and this stronger conscience will increase self-control that can break such strong, bad habits. For this reason, guilt is positive and useful, as long as the values included are not false values.

Guilt is supposed to occur in time to prevent behavior. It is of lesser value *after* the act. Temptation should trigger guilt, which should prevent: failure in main responsibilities (marriage, family, church, employment, etc.); living by wrong values; malingering (laziness, indifference, blaming, faking, pretending, etc.); bad habits; hurting others without just cause.

Recall the case of the married man who had an affair with a much younger woman. He became depressed because his conscience told him he was betraying the highest values of his life, namely, his marriage and family. He also became depressed because he knew his conscience wasn't strong enough to hold his behavior in line with his real life values. He worked through his depression successfully when he strengthened and then heeded his conscience. The worst mistake would have been for a therapist to tell him his values on marriage and family were old-fashioned and misguided and that he should go and have a good time. The point was that his marriage was his highest value, which his conscience kept telling him. When he got his behavior into line with this highest value, then guilt had performed its proper function and his depression lifted.

Severe Depressions—Are They Always Adaptive or Useful?

Depressions are supposed to give messages about needed character change and situation change. Depressions are very useful if their messages result in necessary changes. But what if the person fails to accomplish the change? Severe depressions often give very difficult messages, such as, "If you want happiness, you are going to have to reconstruct most of your character first." But how do you change the parts which themselves produce change?

Look at these aspects of character: conscience, willpower, self-control, maturity, intelligence, self-esteem. How do you change these building blocks or foundations of character? Only by careful planning, strategy, and awareness.

This book assumes that depressions involve the need to make basic and fundamental changes in personality and character and, further, that severe depressions are always adaptive. But with severe depressions the amount of change required is much greater and goes to the roots of a person's being.

One type of severe depression which does not at first appear to be adaptive is *the depression with many causes.* This multiple-cause depression usually occurs in kind, generous, well-meaning people who do not have a clear idea of what they want out of life. Consequently, they go along with the ideals and pursuits of family and friends, ending up depressed because of a loss of meaning and personal identity. These depressions do not appear to be adaptive because they lack an easily identifiable single cause of depression. But many small causes can, and often do, put as much pressure on a person as one major cause can do. These depressions are, in fact, adaptive, but they are difficult to understand because of the many messages about change, rather than the usual one or two.

Another severe depression which does not appear to be adaptive is the depression which has persisted for years. These persistent depressions have given the message to change but the person has failed to accomplish the change. The failure has added further distress, so that the person is now getting a double message: "You must change, but whenever you try to change, it results in failure." Many such depressions go in circles—"I must succeed, I must change. But when I try to change, I fail. When I fail, I get more depressed." This is part of what it means to be depressed about being depressed. These circular depressions often last for years. No depressed person needs further failures, and these failures should be avoided if possible. Every failure is dangerous because it can deepen depression. For this reason every attempt to succeed must be planned carefully to ensure its success.

Some depressions appear to be in the middle area between the medical-biochemical depressions and the character-situation depressions. However, a careful look at these depressions usually shows that they are not in the middle area. Rather, they involve both types of depression at once. The person usually has a clinical-medical depression but is also psychologically depressed about being biochemically depressed. In this case the adaptive message about this double depression is the need for both medical and psychological help to resolve it.

In the chapters that follow, we will explain the most basic and fundamental areas of character change: beliefs, values, goals, habits, emotional openness and honesty, assertiveness, anxiety, and self-control. These basic areas of character are the main emphases of the book. Do not expect success in making such basic changes to come either quickly or easily. But the effort is worth the while. Big improvements can come from basic changes. Give it your best try.

Self-Help Is Sometimes Not Enough!

A final word about severe and long-lasting depressions. Self-help may not be enough. This self-help guide may be of great value to most who have characterological and situational depressions, but some will also benefit from professional help from a mental health expert or pastor-counselor. If early childhood experiences were frightening, degrading, confusing, abusive, it may be that a trained counselor can help with the unraveling and sorting out that is part of depression resolution. Get whatever help you need. Do not go it alone if the load is too heavy to bear. And get the help soon!

Do You Have Confidence in God's Creative Work?

The adaptive view of depression gives a score of 100 percent to the design and perfection of all of God's creative work, especially God's creation of the human mind. It is wrong to view His creative work with negativism and doubt. He made man capable of *anger,* because anger is so necessary and constructive when it is directed by a good conscience and sound reason. He made man capable of *sorrow* over losses, simply because man must value his life and family, and he must have sorrow over the loss of any great value. God made man capable of *guilt,* because guilt is the foremost necessary and constructive emotion when it is motivated by true beliefs and sound values. *Fear* comes in the same category of being necessary and constructive, as long as it is rational. Each of these emotions is necessary and wholesome when appropriate and directed by sound reason.

Then why do some people consider *anger* to be evil, when, in fact, it is often good and only sometimes evil, depending on the persons involved in the situation? "If you are angry, do not let anger lead you into sin" (Eph. 4:26). Mature people do get angry, but they express their anger righteously with good judgment and control.

Guilt takes a prize as a very constructive emotion, in spite of what Sigmund Freud said to the contrary. Never try to reduce guilt unless it is based on wrong values or false beliefs. Instead, bolster conscience and direct guilt so that conduct is always in line with your highest values. Guilt is God's way of getting us to accept high standards and live by them. Only when guilt is out of proportion and based on wrong values should it be replaced. God made no mistake when He made us capable of sorrow, anger, fear, and guilt. God made no mistake when He made us capable of depression, and we have a responsibility to work through depression successfully to become the better person we need to be.

God has created your mind with potential to learn, remember, solve problems, and think. But He leaves it to you to create and be responsible for your own character. So pick your beliefs, values, attitudes, and habits wisely, because together they make up your character. If you make any unwise choices about character, depression may result until you correct these unwise choices. Depression is God's choice of a built-in mechanism to get you to tend to self-growth and self-improvement whenever it is necessary.

4
Depression→ Character Change→ Self Esteem

We Create Our Own Character!

Character is the sum total of a person's guiding principles, beliefs, and values. These principles and beliefs of character are *not inherited* genetically. Rather, we consciously create our own character throughout childhood and adulthood by actively choosing our preference of those principles and beliefs we see around us. When a child decides to steal or not to steal, he is creating that part of his character, and for the rest of his life he may retain that part or may re-create his character at any time by rejecting the principle of stealing for some other principle. Life itself, for most people, is the continuous process of strengthening character; and most older persons, having worked at character growth for many years, find there is still much character building yet to be done.

Look at these basic guiding principles, beliefs, and values. How do they fit into your character?

1. *Accepting or denying reality* (How much will I face facts squarely, and how much will I fake, pretend, manipulate others, and fool myself?)

2. *Accepting or denying self* (Is there a good and wholesome meaning of selfishness? Am I selfish in this positive sense?)

3. *Accepting or denying personal responsibility* (Can I go on blaming others forever?)

4. *Accepting or denying the proper rule of reason over emotion* (If it feels good, should I do it? Or should I do what I think is right even if I don't feel like doing it?)

5. *Accepting or rejecting the principle of cause and effect* (Does everything in my life have a rational explanation? Am I the main cause for my character and the direction of my life?)

6. *Accepting or denying my own mind as the value of my life* (How seriously should I take the opinions and preferences of others? Should I shape my life in the image of my own highest values, and then let the chips fall where they may? How much should I let others determine my character?)

From the above list of *character principles,* and from the questions that these principles answer, it should be very clear that *character is not inherited.* Each person creates his own character and then re-creates it as often as he chooses, reaffirms, or changes his guiding principles. *We create our own character,* and we are fully responsible for it. We always have the choice to keep our character as is or to change it.

The popular view of character, which is wrong, says that character can be blamed on parents, peers, and society. "When I was three, my mother ran away with her lover! And so it follows that everything I do that's wrong is someone else's fault." But blaming is looking backward and never leads to inner growth. Instead of blaming others, the depressed person must accept the responsibility for change and improvement in his own self. Blame only turns others against us, and makes it even harder for us to work to change ourselves.

Depression Aims at Character Change!

Depression is adaptive! And what does "adaptive" mean? *Adaptive* means: useful, life-serving, life-preserving, and of positive value. Depression is adaptive because of its positive function of pointing us to critical areas of our life that are in need of repair and improvement. These critical areas can be *external:* in our relationships, in our employment, in our social life; but these critical areas can also be *internal,* especially character weaknesses. If the critical area is internal, then the purpose of the depression is character change, in which our mental energy and ability are used to replace character weaknesses with character strengths. It is a beautiful thing to see a person struggle to upgrade his character by conscious choice of higher values and stronger life principles.

Character Change Is Hard Work

Character change is hard work in several different ways:

1. It takes much thinking to figure out just what is wrong, and this thinking is definitely work. Have you noticed how some people cannot sleep at night even after the lights are out and everyone else is quietly in bed? They cannot sleep because they are thinking. Ideally, this thinking is the hard work of careful situational or character analysis, aimed at fully understanding what is wrong and why. The reason the mind is active at night is the quietness and freedom from interruption, which often results in our deepest and most rational thinking.

2. Character weaknesses, such as "being too passive," are extremely *complex*, and they usually include a number of entrenched bad habits, negative attitudes, and negative thinking. To see the character weakness clearly is to see all the ways it influences our behavior, and each weakness works like a "ripple effect," by spreading out to touch other areas of our personality. The following diagram illustrates the ripple effect of passivity.

3. To change the character weakness into a character strength requires that you *change the values*, the *habits*, the *attitudes*, and the *thinking* that go with it. You must fight the battle of change on more than one front at the same time if you are going to win. That is very hard to do.

4. Another important reason that character change is such hard work is that *other people don't want us to change*. They may even have trained us to be this way, as in the case of a husband whose own mother was dominated, and now he has trained his wife to accept his domination. When his wife wants to change her character and stands up for herself and talks back, he sees her efforts as a real setback for him. Another example: The wife is slowly maturing and working hard at character growth, but the husband wants her to be the same

THE RIPPLE EFFECT OF CHARACTER WEAKNESS

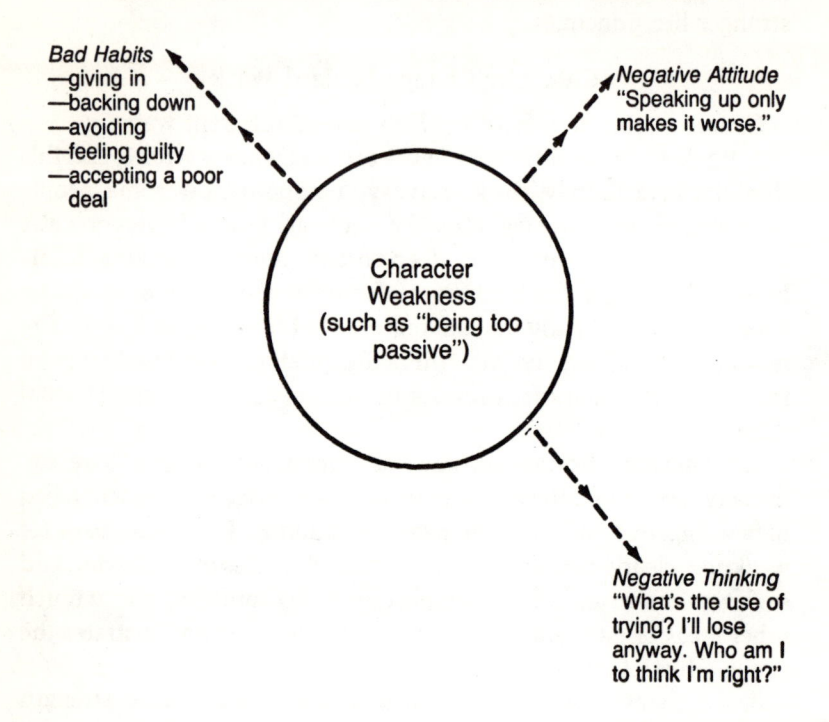

Bad Habits
—giving in
—backing down
—avoiding
—feeling guilty
—accepting a poor deal

Negative Attitude
"Speaking up only makes it worse."

Character Weakness (such as "being too passive")

Negative Thinking
"What's the use of trying? I'll lose anyway. Who am I to think I'm right?"

person he married twenty-five years ago. He hasn't changed, and neither should she. Another example: The battle of adolescents for their freedom is a serious problem because both parents are in the rut of careful supervision and control of their children. Then when the children become adolescents, the parents want to turn the clock back and continue to treat them as children. Employers, employees, lovers, spouses, parents, sons and daughters, friends—any or all of these may feel comfortable with you the way you are, even if you are not satisfied with yourself; and they can be counted on to try to prevent some of the changes you desire in yourself. It's not surprising that some marriages break up and some children rebel. Who wants to be tied forever to one's present shape and size when personal growth is so exciting and necessary for life?

Self-Hate Sometimes Helps Character Change!

Because there are well-known examples of destructive hate, we tend to forget the basic truth that, when it is properly aimed and controlled, hate can be a constructive emotion. Consider how hatred of slavery, hatred of ignorance, hatred of poverty, hatred of disease, and hatred of weakness have spurred heroes to make the world a better place to live.

Self-hate is usually constructive, too! But it is important to note the difference between "hating parts of self" and "hating my whole self." If self-hate means hating my character weaknesses, then it can become a force for positive change. Example: A person begins to hate being fat, and his shape appears ugly to him. He begins to hate his weak willpower, which does not help him enough to resist the temptation to eat. He hates going shopping for new clothes, because it is an embarrassment. These forms of hate can all be constructive. But if he then gets a self-hate complex, he starts to hate his character strengths, too, and his thinking changes so that he mistakenly sees flaws, defects, weaknesses, and inadequacies wherever he takes a look at himself. In this example, self-hate started out as a corrective influence because the self-hate was properly directed at a genuine weakness. To this degree, self-hate could lead to positive character change, as there was recognition that the hated parts of self were causing much unhappiness and must be changed. The problem is to limit and control hate and keep it from spreading and spilling over. Don't hate yourself for hating yourself, as long as you can remember and appreciate your good points, too. Don't be caught up in hate; rather, give hate a proper task by focusing your self-hate constructively on only one character weakness at a time, even though this one character weakness will be related to various bad habits and attitudes.

Self-Esteem Is Liking Your Character

Self-esteem is a confidence and satisfaction with one's own character, even if there is still much room for improvement. Remember that we create our own character, and we certainly are stuck with the character we have created unless or until we change it. But self-esteem is looking at this character you have created and deciding you did a fairly good job on it. You are still working to improve your character, but you can live quite well with it as is.

Ideally, self-esteem is a person liking oneself. Note that it is not self-love, which has some unwillingness to admit flaws and weaknesses. But it is *self-liking,* meaning we add up our character strengths in one column and our character weaknesses in another column. As we compare the two totals, we are pleased that the strengths more than balance out the weaknesses. Basically, with self-esteem, we appreciate the good in us and tolerate the weaknesses, while at the same time striving to turn them into character strengths.

Self-Esteem Has to Be Earned

Low self-esteem is not a problem in itself, and hopefully it leads to positive character changes. But a serious crisis occurs (depression itself!) if we try to change our character and fail in the attempt. Our low self-esteem drops even lower than before. Some depressives have failed every time, and now they feel helpless to achieve the desired changes. Though they are depressed, perhaps for many years, and want very much to change, they now refuse to think, struggle, and persist in a course of action that might lead to the desired changes.

This type of depression, which is a crisis of low self-esteem, can be overcome. This chapter, and in fact this entire book, gives strategies or techniques for overcoming these characterological depressions. But there is no substitute for success, and you must succeed in your efforts at character change in order to achieve lasting appropriate self-esteem.

Self-esteem has to be earned, and the only way of earning self-

Depression Should Lead to Character Change

esteem is by succeeding in necessary character changes. Let us consider, in very brief form, the best ways of achieving self-esteem:

1. Analyze your depression adequately. If the depression is due to disastrous life circumstances, then you must restructure your life to adjust to the disaster. If the depression is due to a character weakness, you must overcome that weakness. Is your depression due to life events or character weakness or both?

2. Chapters 5 to 11 give specific solutions to the common types of character weakness:
- Base Your Life on True Beliefs and Sound Values
- Think and Reason Clearly
- Increase Self-Control
- Update Your Life Goals and Revive Your Enthusiasm
- Turn Anxiety into Motivation
- Express Your Emotions
- Be Assertive

Now is the time to look at this list of ways to work on character change and select one area (at a time) to which you will give priority in your effort at character change. Then turn to the chapter on that topic, and get to work.

Self-esteem, then, is a confidence and satisfaction in one's own character, even if there is still much room for growth and improvement. But self-esteem must be earned by success in character change, as a person works to shape his character in the image of his highest values and senses he is succeeding in doing so.

3. Shyness can be a special problem. Shyness normally makes us sensitive to the opinions of others and challenges us to achieve their approval. But in its extreme form it exaggerates the importance of the opinions of others and makes our self-esteem depend on the esteem others have for us.

To recover from this exaggeration of the value of the opinions of others, learn to devalue the opinions of others. Their opinions may be right or wrong, just as your own opinions may be right or wrong. The more important matter is to have your own opinions and to express them. Being right or wrong is rarely critical and final because we have the opportunity to change our opinions if we decide we are wrong.

Depression ⟶ Character Change ⟶ Self-Esteem

We are discussing a process of human nature which starts at depression and ends at self-esteem. What comes in between is character change, and character change is the heart of the matter. And you **can change,** with hard work, patience, persistence, common sense, humility, and good strategy.

Life cannot be better if it remains the same. Change is necessary if life is going to improve. The past must *not* provide the pattern for the future. You must think, reason, and decide what you want your life to become. You must plan and act so that your desires are fulfilled. You must become the kind of person you know you ought to become; then you will have self-esteem.

Tuum Est. Remember this Latin phrase? It means: "The outcome of this battle is entirely up to you."

Part 2
Change Your Depressive Thinking

5
Live by True Beliefs and Sound Values

This chapter looks at beliefs and values that lead out of depression. It assumes that false beliefs and wrong values are often causes of depressions.

Accepting Reality, Or, A Is A

This is Aristotle's principle of identity or noncontradiction, and it is probably the greatest depression fighter of all. It says that a spade is always a spade, so why call it something else? Manipulation is manipulation, and when people are manipulating you, don't try to find a sugarcoating to cover it up. Relationships are what they are, not what others are faking or pretending them to be. Reality is reality, and it is rarely hard to figure out if we use our own minds and ignore the mental games and dishonest secret strategies of others to control and use us unfairly. It is often difficult to accept reality, but it is not so difficult to figure it out.

When we have the facts and reason clearly, there are never contradictions. Trust your own mind and believe what it is telling you. Come to your own conclusions. Do your own thinking. There are absolutes, and these absolutes apply in all events and circumstances. Never fool yourself into faking reality, and never let another person fog or smoke screen what the issues are. Example? A husband talks of true love and faithfulness, but his actions are the opposite. This contradiction is only in the words, not in reality. The reality is his actions.

Brutal honesty with oneself is the first step down the road that leads out of depression. Call a spade a spade. Analyze your relationships by the facts, not the facade, and admit to yourself exactly where you are now standing. You can't get going in the direction that is *right* for you until you admit to yourself exactly the direction you are already going.

A is A, whether we like it or not. Accept reality.

Accepting Self, Or, Selfishness Is Often Good

My only responsibility is to make my life conform to the image of my highest ideals, whatever these may be. It is my life, and these are my ideals. My life is my responsibility. All of my relationships with others must exist only because it is my judgment that these relationships serve to enhance my life and my ideals. This is the positive view of selfishness. It says I cannot and must not be secondary in any relationship; I must make each relationship secondary to my life and my ideals.

Selfishness sometimes has an ugly and vicious meaning, but it can also be used in this positive sense, meaning that the person never forgets or denies his responsibility to himself. *Self-interest* is a softer word which conveys the positive idea of selfishness.

Depression often means we have lost a noble and honorable sense of self, and we are letting others take charge of our life. Beware of those who teach self-sacrifice, because they often want you to sacrifice your ideals for theirs, and this should never be. All of the normal demands of my relationships must be acceptable to my view of myself as the best person I can be. I must never act on the ideals of my partner or spouse or friend in order to maintain the relationship. The ideals I act upon must always be my ideals, too. Three examples follow:

Self-interested marriage partners often make the best marriages. Each enters the marriage honestly realizing how his/her own highest ideals and interests are enhanced by the marriage. The marriage grows and strengthens as the partners serve themselves; but because it is a voluntary contract of mutual benefit they are at the same time serving the ideals of the partner. Self-sacrifice in marriage is a contradiction and cannot exist. If a devoted husband died trying to rescue his drowning wife, it would be the most self-interested act of his life because he was acting to preserve a great value of his life, namely, his wife.

Depression from the death of a spouse is often a deep and powerful depression. It comes about as the depression serves to loosen and replace this relationship and point us to a new future and new relationships. The depression is the self slowly letting go, which it does only slowly because it is still recoiling from the loss. This depression is based on self-interest and is, for the time being, as it should be, because time is necessary in order to let go of all the benefits of a strong marriage.

Good parenting is often a selfish task, and martyrs make the worst moms. Good parents love their children not only out of a sense of duty, not only because they ought to love them, but because the children are lovable in the parents' eyes. Then, when the children become somewhat unlovable at times for whatever reasons, these parents take constructive action to chip off their children's rough edges and recover the lovable form. But martyr moms ruin this wholesome relationship by helping their children without expecting and demanding any courtesy or kindness in return. "It is my duty as a mother to put my children first ahead of me, and I should not expect anything in return," they say. This nonsense of putting children first turns children into such spoiled, irresponsible, inconsiderate persons that even a mother would find them hard to love. Every good mother should expect and demand from her children the minimum payment of common courtesy and appreciation and respect. In addition, every good mother should expect and demand that every child assume his or her fair share, depending on age and size, of the household and family responsibilities. Whenever the children refuse these courtesies and responsibilities, parents must reason, explain, discipline, go on strike, or do whatever is necessary to return the parent-child relationship to a mutual benefit, not simply a benefit to the child. Many parents are seriously depressed because their unselfish parenting has created a monster, and the depression demands that parents insist upon this monster changing back into an acceptable family member.

Accepting Responsibility, Or, the Outcome Is Up to You

Tuum est—"It is entirely up to you" was a phrase used by Roman soldiers to spur the troops before battle. "The outcome of this battle is entirely up to you," the general shouted, and the sound of his voice carried out over the listening soldiers; but he knew they didn't believe him. They thought the gods of Roman mythology decided battles. While the general was speaking, they looked at cloud formations or wind changes or the innards of animals to try to foresee their fate in battle.

But the troops were wrong: *Tuum est* is true, and individuals determine their own destiny by their thoughts, values, decisions, efforts, and skills. Each person must paddle his own canoe, and how well he does it, the direction picked, the reading of river rapids and weather conditions, and all the relevant factors will determine how the voyage goes. Luck is neither for us nor against us, so we cannot just wait for our luck to change; we have to make our luck.

I have to make my life work. It's not up to anyone else. I have to think, move, speak, decide, and react, and I have to put all of this together into a workable, satisfying life. My life is entirely up to me, not to chance and fortune.

My happiness is not the responsibility of my spouse. Can you believe the incredible wife who said to her husband, "It is up to you to make me happy—now do it!" Spouses owe one another only mutual respect, mutual love, mutual sharing, but each is still responsible for his or her own state of mind, mood, and life.

My life is not up to parents, children, employers, institutions, or governments. The world owes no one a living or even a single helping hand. Your life is in your own hands, and it's your own responsibility, so get going.

Your brother is *not* your keeper, except briefly in time of emergency. You must support your own life by a good day's work and by the effort of your mind.

You are depressed? Fine. Now it is entirely up to you to work through your depression successfully by determination and cunning and whatever else you can do to help yourself. Take over and start controlling your life, and you will be started on the way out of depression. Whatever you do, stop blaming others and the world. Take the responsibility for your life and enjoy it.

Accepting Cause, Effect, and Reason—Or, Everything Has a Rational Explanation

There is a great principle called the law of cause and effect, which is a valuable tool in working through depressions. This law states that everything that happens, however small or large, can be fully explained by analyzing what caused it to happen that way. For instance, what causes three sons who grew up in the same family to develop so differently? Is there a cause?

Is there an answer to such a question, or is it unexplainable? Is there a reason or must it forever be a mystery? The law of cause and effect says that the full answer is there in the causes that influenced the three sons, if only someone will search for these causes.

Reason is the law of cause and effect as it applies to the mind. Reason is not content to analyze and explain only the past in terms of causes. Reason looks to the future to predict what can be done now in the family of the three sons while they are still infants so that they will grow and develop attitudes and skills that will help them in their adult life. Reason is the search for ways to bring about these desirable changes. Reason insists that human life moves and flows and develops only by the reliable and logical law of cause and effect, not by chance, not by luck, not by mystery, and certainly not by the unexplainable.

Another aspect of the law of cause and effect is the hope and confidence it gives to those who decide to live by reason. Why does reason give confidence? Because it tells us that problems are solvable, difficulties can be overcome, and life can move forward. Reason tells us what we can and cannot do in order to make the changes we want. We can know which problems are solvable and which are not by the use of reason; then we can spend all of our mental energy on the solvable ones.

What is the relationship between reason and depression? Depression is our emotions prodding us to use reason to focus on our problems and solve them. As reason works to understand the problems of individuals, marriages, families, businesses, and even empires, it reveals the steps to correct these problems and thus resolve the depression. Depression is emotions, but it is only resolved by reason. Because every aspect of life—movement, a sound, a thought, a process, a relationship, a society, or a civilization—must, if it is capable of being understood at all, be understood by reason alone, then every aspect of a depression can also be understood by reason alone. Reason alone can point to the way that leads out of depression.

Here are some familiar sayings that restate and elaborate the law of cause and effect:
- Whatever you sow, you shall reap.
- If you play with fire, you will get burned.
- Ask, and you will receive.
- Pride cometh before a fall.
- If you don't work, you won't eat.
- Spare the rod, and spoil the child.
- Sleeping at harvesttime means hunger in the spring.
- A soft answer turneth away wrath.
- A stitch in time saves nine.
- A penny saved is a penny earned.
- Sow on good ground and you may receive a hundredfold.
- A rolling stone gathers no moss.

Study these sayings and see, in each of them, the invitation to you to take control of your life and make your life what you want it to be.

Accepting Individuality, Or, I Am Alone

Have you been overrating the importance of relationships and forgetting that for the most part humans live alone with only their thoughts and desires as company? No, we are not grizzly bears who travel alone and come together only to breed. Yes, we humans are social animals who mate for life and live together in families and communities. But it is a mistake to overrate relationships and to make

Change Your Depressive Thinking

our focus social rather than personal. Sound mental health comes from being on very good terms with your own mind. One road out of depression is the realization that we must, first of all, learn how to enjoy the times we are alone. Time spent alone is the substance or meat of life, while time spent with others is the seasoning or spice. Relationships must be second, and self must be first.

Another aspect of being alone and separate and individual is the fact that unhappiness comes mainly from within us, not from our marriage or family or employment or any social organization. When something does go wrong in any of these relationships, it is obnoxious like a buzzing housefly on a summer's day, but it should not be critical or fatal because we still have the main source of satisfaction which is within us. What is really serious is whether I dislike myself and whether I mistrust myself. Disliking some important parts of self is the deep-rooted source of unhappiness; and if it exists in me, then for my own sake I had better get depressed so I can work through this problem successfully. As long as my problems are in my relationship to others and not within me, I know I can survive and eventually thrive.

Study this list of false beliefs and unsound values to be sure you don't accept them:

I must always take others seriously.
I must depend on others.
I must be loved and appreciated by others at all times.
I must make myself subordinate to my spouse or family.
I have no value and no rights.
Individuals exist for the group.
Mothers exist for their children.
Husbands or wives exist for their spouse.
My mind is not really my own.

All of these false beliefs and unsound values can lead to depression.

Accepting Imperfection, Or, Letting Go of Past Mistakes

The past—yesterday—is gone forever. The past is unimportant except to enjoy pleasant memories and learn from past mistakes. Let the past go, once you have figured it out. Living in the past, reliving past enjoyments, and being preoccupied with past failures and disappointments should take up very little of our time. Depression sometimes focuses on the past but only to figure out what we could have done differently. What is important is the present—we can only live a moment at a time—today. Life really starts over every morning when the new sun comes up.

Failures—they are regrettable and should not be repeated if possible. But failures are also in the past, so learn from them and then move on to better things. To dwell on a failure is to repeat it, because we bring it back from the past and it spoils another moment of time in the present.

Mistakes—these errors or miscalculations are inevitable. Perfection is beyond the reach of all of us. As we make decisions, evaluations, and calculations, we can be right only so much of the time. We must give reasonable care and attention to each step, but mistakes will occur regardless. When they occur, we must note them and then move on. We should also demand that others make allowance for our mistakes; and when they dwell on our mistakes beyond reason, we must refuse to accept this. We must assert our right to make mistakes and take the consequences.

A Philosophy of Life

A philosophy of life is a blend or composite of a person's beliefs, values, attitudes, and goals. A good philosophy helps to make the best of a person, and it turns depressions into opportunities for personal growth. The beliefs and values of the preceding pages have been describing an adaptive or life-serving philosophy, which is now stated in its simplest form:

What is important in the universe is God, fellow humans, and me.

God has made the earth as an ideal place to support life, but

He has made it *neutral.* I must struggle to survive and support myself; and governments, my family, and my fellowman have no obligation to support me. I can count on the natural forces of this planet to be neutral in my struggle to stay alive.

My fellowmen are struggling, too, and they do not owe me a helping hand. They will help me at times and hinder me at other times, but they are mainly *neutral*—and they will neither help me to the shore nor push my head under the water.

Finally, I am happiest, first, when I can find and follow God's purpose and plan for me, and second, when I can live with my fellowmen in peace and harmony. But I owe my fellowmen very little, and I must not let them dictate the terms of my life. I must always struggle to shape my life in the image of my own highest values, not their values.

I must accept God, and search for His purpose for me.

I must accept reality, accept self, and accept responsibility for all of my life, including my depression.

Write Your Own Philosophy of Life

It is important to write a statement of your main guiding principles, beliefs, and values. Try this now, and make a list of your principles. Then ask several friends to look over your list to see if they agree. They may disagree with your self-assessment of your principles, and you should hear them out. Perhaps they can point out some extra principles that you live by. Perhaps they can help you to see some guiding principles which are wrong and which you must work to change. Remember that the key to your depression resolution may be the strengthening or changing of one or more basic principles or beliefs.

6
Think and Reason Clearly

This chapter helps us to detect and correct our own faulty reasoning. It looks first at why we sometimes reason poorly, then at how we can improve our reasoning. Clear thinking leads out of depression.

Good reasoning means finding what good conclusions follow from the available relevant information.

Rule 1—Allow Yourself Enough Time to Think Through the Problem. Don't jump to conclusions. Do not let others pressure you for a quick decision. Good thinkers allow themselves time to weigh the information carefully; they withhold judgment until they have pondered the problem from all angles. The wisest people in the world never have quick, easy answers. Here is what to say when others are hurrying you to decide: "Please allow me more time to think about this, and I'll get back to you about it when I'm ready."

Rule 2—Get Your Emotions in Control Before You Decide. This means you should allow your emotions to have a part in your decision by expressing them honestly to someone before you decide. In this way your emotions simmer down to a level that is compatible with good reason. Emotions should have only a controlled part in your decisions. Good reasoning has a balance of reason and emotion.

Rule 3—The Rule for Adequate Evidence. This rule says we do not need absolute proof of total evidence in favor of a conclusion, but we do need a reasonable amount of evidence to make the conclusion worthy of being believed. But this evidence must appear as adequate evidence to other reasonable people, or else we are not reasoning properly. We must review and change our conclusion if a quorum of average people evaluate the evidence differently. Example: One man says, "I saw a flying saucer last night near the lake at ten o'clock." Then a group of people speak up and say, "Bill, we saw the flashes of light at the lake last night too, but it was reacting marsh gas, not a flying saucer."

Rule 4—Work Hard at Gathering the Evidence. The evidence is what is important, so dig hard to get the evidence. Do *not* imagine that you are so brilliant that you can have a flashing, sudden, deep insight and understanding that can lead you to the truth quickly and easily without having to work at it carefully and energetically.

Remember *not* to be like the Queen of Hearts in *Alice in Wonderland*, who said, "First let's have the verdict, and then the evidence."

Rule 5—Question Your Biases and Prejudices, and be on guard against them. Good reasoning is based on facts, not on prejudice. A bias exists when you are in favor of something before you have gathered the evidence. A prejudice is a strong bias that prevents you from assessing the facts fairly.

Here is a *fact:* Some native Indians are lazy and alcoholic, but the large majority of native Indians avoid alcohol and prefer a steady job.

Here is a *bias:* I don't know what the statistics are, but I bet you that immigrants to this country are better workers than native Indians.

Here is *prejudice:* All Indians are lazy alcoholics, and I wouldn't even interview a single one to employ.

Rule 6—"This woman has ten children, she's on welfare, and she needed the money; so I think it is only fair that you, the jury, find her innocent." This is *the appeal to pity,* and it is a false argument. Do not come to a particular conclusion simply because you feel sorry for a person.

Rule 7—Fallacies of Ambiguity. Ambiguity means the meaning or trend of the information is not clear. If the evidence is not clear, we cannot fairly come to a conclusion. We have to withhold judgment. Example: One person says, "Oil pollution is killing our fish and wildlife, so vote for the antipollution candidate." Another person must answer, "First, what do you mean by pollution? Second, what is your evidence?"

Rule 8—Don't believe something just because there is no evidence against it. Beliefs and conclusions need real supporting evidence, not simply a lack of conflicting evidence.

Rule 9—Don't Be Swayed by the Majority View. You want the evidence, not a Gallup poll or consensus. Ignore such slogans as "One billion Chinese Communists can't be wrong," because of course they could all very well be wrong about Communism and probably are!

Rule 10—Do Not Favor the Underdog, or minority view. Instead, let the facts decide. "Well, I'm for C. P. Rail because it is smaller and privately owned, and C. N. Railways is too big and is government backed."

Rule 11—Begging the Question means to avoid answering a question for proof by saying, "That question does not deserve an answer because everyone knows the answer is obvious and true."

Example: Question: "Why do you attend church?" Begging the question: "Well, if you don't know the answer, there is no point in myexplaining, as you wouldn't understand anyway."

Rule 12—The Fallacy of Guilt By Association or Character Defamation. This false view attacks a person's conclusions because of some supposed undesirable characteristic. "Don't believe anyone over thirty." "Don't believe Bertrand Russell's view of science because he was a pacifist and he believed in free love." "We must reject the theory of relativity as false, for its author is Albert Einstein, and Einstein is a Jew." These are examples of faulty reasoning of guilt by association.

Rule 13—Innocence by Association. "We can trust his judgment because he is a good friend of Jack and Sally, who are good people." More faulty reasoning.

Rule 14—The Appeal to Authority. "Football coach of the year, Thug Cleats, believes that God exists, so it must be so." "Robinson, who is an authority on this matter, says so; therefore, it must be true." "There is no need to argue that a woman's place is in the home, because tradition speaks for itself." More faulty reasoning.

Analyzing Our Own Thinking

If we are fooling ourselves, we are heading for unhappiness, frustration, and disappointment. But we may not know we are fooling ourselves! Study this list of questions which will help us to be more honest:

1. Are we *afraid to change* some of our views just because we have held them for so long? Yet things cannot be different for us unless we change our views.

2. Are we *in a mental rut,* because we stopped doing serious thinking years ago and now we are left marooned in our outdated, old-fashioned views and values?

3. Are we *lazy,* and we can't be bothered to make the effort to bring our life up-to-date after a twenty-year "sleep"?

4. Are we *procrastinators,* who keep saying we will get around to a mental overhaul, but not just yet? And we never really intend to make any changes.

5. Are we *refusing to face the fact of the sorry state of our lives?*

6. Are we *honest* with ourselves about our outlook for the future?

7. Are we *wishing we were younger again,* instead of accepting our age and its opportunities?

In what parts of your life are you fooling yourself by your unclear thinking?

Tuum est—it is entirely up to you to get your thinking straightened out! This Latin phrase means you can't blame others for all the mess you find yourself in.

Straight-Thinking Christians

The world certainly needs more straight-thinking Christians. Christians are the salt of the earth when they think straight, but they often tumble into depression when they are muddled and befuddled.

Families need Christian parents to think straight about parenting, and the world needs these straight-thinking Christian families. But failures in parenting—by permissiveness or by abusive strictness— can bring a Christian parent to his knees with severe depression. The children from such families also become depressed, and with good reason, because *permissiveness* builds in unrealistic hopes and expectations which are soon disappointed and because *abusive strictness* breeds skepticism and loss of Christian faith which, in turn, produces depression.

Congregations also need straight thinking if they are to have that progressive and wholesome outreach that Christ would have them achieve. Straight-thinking congregations have won entire communities to faith in Christ and to plant countless new congregations. The Kingdom has always prospered by this Christ-centered and congregation-centered approach. But what sadness to observe depressed congregations, who have all the signs of depressed individuals— *pessimism* (isn't it preposterous that the servants of the sovereign God should be pessimistic about the future of a New Testament congregation *if* it is thinking straight?), *lack of energy, confusion, wrong attitudes, wrong goals.* May God give us congregations who have *confidence* (faith) to persist in their spiritual battles. Straight thinking can lead congregations to this kind of confidence.

Part 3
Change Your Depressive Behavior

Part 4
Change Your Depressive Behavior

7
Increase Self-Control

Riding the Wild Horses

In the eastern foothills of the Rockies are small herds of wild horses. These horses are beautiful, free, healthy, strong, and useless. They cannot carry a rider safely to a destination. They cannot pull a plow or wagon. Their strength and energy is abundant, but is good only for running, eating, fighting, and breeding.

However, from time to time ranchers round up these horses and, using a great deal of knowledge, skill, and strategy, train them for riding and work. The whole purpose of this training is to get complete control of the animal without breaking its spirit. To do this requires several steps:

1. Get the animal's *trust* by gradually getting closer and closer to the animal without frightening it or hurting it.

2. Get the animal's *affection* by feeding, watering, grooming, talking, and giving affection.

3. Get the animal's *obedience* by saddling and riding the animal, while it is bucking, until it finally stops from defeat and exhaustion.

4. Train the animal.

A good horse trainer is fascinating to watch because his knowledge, skill, and strategy all combine to get the horse trained with the least time, the least energy, the least danger, for the best possible, longest-lasting results.

Another type of trainer is a dog trainer, whose goal is to get the animal's complete obedience, but without interfering with the dog's own happiness. Think of how much a family can enjoy a pet which keeps the rules of the family but still runs and romps around and fully enjoys its life within the reasonable limits placed upon it.

Well-trained horses and well-trained dogs are like people who have adequate self-control. Adequate self-control means that people are able to exercise restraint over their urges, impulses, and desires; and they follow a moderate course of action that is not extreme or excessive. They regulate themselves to keep within limits. They still feel the urges and impulses, but they control them. They are still tempted, but they resist the temptation. In the language of horse training, these self-controlled persons have "tamed their wild urges" and put them in the service of lifelong goals, not urges of the moment.

Are you in charge of your life? Do you put your energy and ability to work for you, or are you controlled by urges, impulses, and habits that can only bring momentary pleasure and long-term misery? Do you need to ride and tame your own inner wild horses? Are you depressed because you are not fully in control of yourself? Depression can come because we are not controlling our impulses and habits, and they are controlling us.

Are any of these impulses or habits running your life and making you depressed?

1. Overeating (you are overweight, and are now trying your thirty-first diet without success)
2. Smoking
3. Abusing alcohol
4. Gambling
5. Stealing or dishonesty
6. Laziness
7. Faking, pretending, and manipulating in relationships
8. Passivity or aggression, insulting, pettiness
9. Over spending
10. Superficial
11. Irresponsible
12. Other _____
_____
_____

This is a chapter on gaining self-control and the steps to take to achieve it:

(1) Self-control has to be a battle to the finish and this means total *commitment* to change.

(2) Study the area of your life where you wish to gain control until you have complete *awareness* of all its features.

(3) Develop a *strategy* for control.

Commitment

We are all such creatures of habit that we must pick our habits very carefully as though we were going to have them for a lifetime. The popularity of the saying, "You can't teach an old dog new tricks," shows how hard it is for adults to change their ways. This is a true saying because it is difficult for adults to change; and without commitment or determination to change, change will not occur.

Commitment is the willpower, determination, and resolve to do something even if it costs us frustration, pain, inconvenience, money, and time. Commitment involves counting the cost first. It means that we expect it will be a tough road ahead, with temptation and other negative features. But we want something badly enough that we will endure whatever suffering or discomfort is necessary in order to get control. We will not give up and retreat the first time we stumble or slip back. We will not give up the fight, even if we lose some battles. We will keep on fighting to the finish. We will anticipate setbacks, obstacles, and further failures, but we will keep on struggling until we get the self-control we desire.

Complete Control Yokum—This Li'l Abner comic strip character had complete control over himself most of the time. Life has to be this way. Commitment is the first step toward believing firmly that self-control is good. You are determined to sacrifice something short-term, some momentary pleasures for your long-term happiness and best interest.

Commitment involves *priorities,* or placing things at the top of our list of things to do first and doing the rest only afterward. Self-control must be a top priority if it is to be reached. It must come before leisure, hobbies, reading the newspaper, and watching TV. What are your priorities?

Here is an example of Sally's commitment:

> There I was twenty years of age, and drifting whichever way the wind or current took me. As a child I had never needed to organize myself and take charge of my life because my mother always stood over me and made me do my work. When she did this, my only effort was to resist her and try to scramble her attempts to get me to be self-directed. I never made any serious effort to get control of my impulses—that was Mother's job.
>
> What a great day it was for me, though I cried at the time, when my boyfriend, Bob, ended our relationship. I knew I had lost him because I was too lax, easygoing, and directionless. Even for him, I had been unable to get my act together. He said, "Sally, I have a lot of fun when we go out to a party, but the fact is that we don't think alike." He was right, of course, because he was serious, working with single-mindedness to reach the goals he had set for himself. And there I was, all 185 pounds of me at five-foot-eight. I liked to eat, so I ate. I liked to drive fast, so I did. I didn't like to study my college course, so I didn't. My urges and impulses ran my life, and my self-discipline was nearly zero. Goodbye, Bob.
>
> So guess whose shoulder I went to cry on? You guessed it—good old Mom! Only this time I was a big loser. Mom was also shocked about my losing Bob. I said, "Mom, I was a fool to resist you when you tried to organize me so that *my mind would control my impulses,* not my impulses control my mind. Now I can see that style of living is best for me in the long run so I am going after it, regardless of the cost, until it is the new me."

Awareness

Awareness means that we carefully study the part of our life we want to change. We analyze each act, each movement, and each feeling into its component parts. To analyze something is to itemize all of its causes and their interrelationships. We must increase our knowledge of our bad habit or impulse until we become an expert on that subject. As we analyze ourselves, we pull out of our subconscious all of the reasons why we do it that particular way, until finally the subconscious is conscious. This is another definition of awareness: consciousness or making the subconscious to be conscious.

Do you want to gain control of your eating habits and maintain your ideal weight for the rest of your life? You will never accomplish this with commitment only. You must also have awareness of all aspects of weight control, including your own eating habits, caloric values of foods, reasons for overeating, and health aspects of being overweight. Study the following examples of new awareness that led to new self-control:

1. "I discovered I was getting most of my fat from snacking with the kids in front of the TV. Knowing this, I made myself a simple rule: No snacking whatever in the evenings until the kids are all in bed at 9:30."

2. "I discovered that my weight was high because of my passion for bread and potatoes, so I limited myself to one slice of bread per day and one medium potato per day (restaurant meals, picnics, and snacks included)."

3. "I discovered that my anxiety and tension with my wife started each evening with driving the car home from work in heavy traffic. I was already tense from driving when I walked into the house. When we started jogging and showering together before supper as soon as I got home, with no complaints from either person until we had finished supper, what a difference it made."

4. "I became aware that I was yelling at the children mainly because Dad had always yelled at me. My yelling was just as useless as Dad's had been. So when the kids came in from school, I set my oven timer for thirty minutes, and then allowed myself no yelling and no negative remarks until the timer told me the thirty minutes was up, by which time I was thinking positive from thirty minutes of conscious self-control of my yelling."

5. "I learned that I was passive partly because my parents were passive, but mostly because I could fool myself into thinking things would straighten out by themselves. Knowing this about myself, I

knew I had to straighten out my own mind first, and then I had to radically and actively intrude into each situation to make it what I wanted it to be. When I learned my attitude was the problem, I knew what to do about it."

In each of these examples, people studied themselves, their habits, their impulses, their reasoning, and their backgrounds. They analyzed and then set themselves to make changes. This is the secret of increasing our awareness.

Strategy

If you want to build a sod shack, you don't need elaborate architectural drawings, and you don't need a foundation—you simply start cutting and piling the sod to make walls, and the bare ground is already there for a floor. The tallest sod shack ever built was in Kentucky, and the walls were eleven feet high. Is your life like a sod shack in that it is simple, small, without a firm foundation, and without planning? Strategy is planning to achieve a goal.

Skyscrapers require steel-reinforced cement in the foundation, which must reach down to bedrock. The building blueprints must be exact to one eighth of an inch, and they must cover every aspect of the building and meet stringent regional building codes.

Planning includes financial planning, heating, plumbing, electrical, air conditioning, parking, earthquake considerations, fire safety, and many other aspects. Is your life like a skyscraper in that you plan wisely and you believe that problems can be overcome by strategy, planning, and good management?

Most of us are somewhere in between the sod shack and the skyscraper. We work hard to keep ahead of the problems that arise, and we are still able to reserve energy and thought to plan for improvements in life. We have learned that good strategy is half of self-control.

What strategies lead to greater self-control?

1. Write down your personal philosophy of life. This should include: (a) Main beliefs about your own independence and your major relationships; (b) your view of just how much you think you

Change Your Depressive Behavior

should take others seriously; and (c) your view of just how much you think the world owes you and just how much you owe the world. Your philosophy should emphasize independence and self-sufficiency, or else it will result in inadequate self-control and recurring depressions.

2. Set immediate, intermediate, and long-term goals for your life. Read the chapter on goals and the sound planning that helps us reach them.

3. Check your beliefs and values. They must be true, consistent, and reasonable. Reread the chapter on beliefs and values.

4. Be emotive, be assertive, and relax. Read these three chapters. You can't achieve effective self-control without these three personality characteristics.

5. Use your *new awareness* to see the logical consequences that point to strategy. The strategy ought to fit naturally and appropriately to you and the situation you face, like a suit or dress that is tailor-made. Study cause and effect and figure out what strategy (or cause) will produce the desired results (or effect).

6. Change is the goal of strategy. You can't have change if you want everything to remain the same. Ask yourself what things you want to change. The strategy must aim at change.

7. Force yourself to begin. Set up a timetable or schedule of target dates for achieving the self-control. Knowing when to begin is critical, and you can start too quickly (before preparations are complete) or too late (and the opportunity may have passed). Don't jump the gun, and don't dawdle at the starting gate.

8. If possible, work out strategies aimed at one problem at a time. Concentrate your energies. Andrew Carnegie (Canny Andy) used to say, "Put all your eggs in one basket, and then watch that basket." Don't attempt too many changes at once. Focus in on one area of self-control at a time.

9. Enlist the experts to help you in developing strategies. They are there to help—psychologists, bankers, pastors, priests, medical doctors, social workers. Borrowing ideas and proven strategies for self-control is learning from the successes and mistakes of others. There is no easier way to find good strategies.

10. Reward yourself frequently for your first signs of growth in self-control. Rewards make us eager to succeed some more. They are the best motivators.

11. Enlist the help of organizations: churches, Weight Watchers, Alcoholics Anonymous, self-help groups.

12. Take courses in the areas in which you need to grow.

Self-Control Is Only One Ability Among Many

Some Christian groups have raised the ability of self-control above the other abilities. "If you get self-control, the other abilities come easy," they say. In some ways this is true: Self-control is special as it was in the life of the apostle Paul. However, other special abilities are necessary: Barnabas was gracious and forgiving, Timothy was cooperative and conciliatory, Moses was the meekest man on earth, and John was full of love. The world needs a few people in whom self-control is the special gift, but most of us need to have balance and moderation in our personal and social skills. Yet Peter tells us, "You must therefore be mentally stripped for action, perfectly self-controlled" (1 Pet. 1:13).

8
Update Your Life Goals and Revive Enthusiasm

Rethink Your Past and Future

Depression gets us to think over the meaning of our life, in order to make improvements. If a spouse, family member, or close friend dies, we must rethink the past as it was with that person, and we must also rethink the future as it will probably be without that person. If we refuse to think through this person's death, we will probably become depressed until we do. Depression evaluates the significance of the person's death and what changes will result. If a marital separation or loss of job or some failure occurs, we must rethink the past carefully to see the meaning of the loss and to see in what ways we should change to prevent a recurrence of the failure. Again, if we refuse to face this harsh reality, we may become confused and depressed until we face it squarely. Depression in this way gets us to evaluate all possible alternative strategies, alternative attitudes, alternative values, and alternative life-styles. The purpose of evaluating alternatives is to change. Depression is all about the need for change and adjustment to reality. Major changes call for adjustment, and often life cannot go on as it has in the past. Perhaps I can't have a better life unless I act differently. Perhaps I have to change; and if so, then depression leads me to consider *what* and *how* and *when* and *why* to change.

Depression is all about the need for basic major personal changes. The changes may be one or more of the following:
- Change of attitude toward self.
- Change of attitude toward others.

- Breaking bad habits.
- Learning new values as principles of living.
- Learning new skills and habits.
- Finding deeper and richer personal purpose and meaning.
- These are the main changes that lead the way out of depression, and for many depressed persons these changes are the only way out of depression and the only way to personal growth and improvement of life.

Rediscover Enthusiasm

Depression, when left unresolved, can become a habit. We can simply get accustomed to being depressed and learn to live that way. Depression then becomes a rut.

But *enthusiasm,* or zest for living, can also become a habit, a desirable, adaptive habit. The popular true story is often told of a major league baseball player who was fired because he showed no enthusiasm while playing the game. The punchline is that the ballplayer then made up his mind to find another playing job and to earn the reputation as the most enthusiastic baseball player in the major leagues. He got another job and began to force himself to act enthusiastically—regardless of how he actually felt. He ran out on the field on each inning change, instead of slowly dragging himself along. He smiled and waved at the fans and tried to look as if he meant it. He soon began to get the reputation for enthusiasm that he had started out to get; but, to his own surprise and shock, he soon found that his enthusiasm was real and not pretense. Without realizing what he was doing to himself, he had worked himself into the habit of enthusiasm, and he no longer had to put on the act.

This is one of the keys to remotivation. You must break out of the depression rut if that is what you are in. If you force yourself to act enthusiastically every morning until 10:00 AM, you will usually find that you are genuinely enthusiastic for the rest of the day.

A clever way to break the habit of depression is to plan a busy schedule of useful and interesting events—plan a week in advance if you can. Then put your whole heart into the schedule and be ready for the pleasant surprise of a new mood and happier days.

The Right Goals and Enthusiasm

To recover our motivation and enthusiasm, it is valuable to discuss, review, clarify, and revise our goals. All goals need this careful consideration, whether they are short-term, intermediate, long-term, or lifetime goals. Look at the following table of goals that hold us in a depression and goals that lead us out of a depression.

Types of Goals

Goals that Depress	*Goals that Lead Us Out of Depression*
Unclear goals	*Clear* goals
Conflicting goals	*Compatible* goals
Illogical goals	*Sound and reasonable* goals
Self-sacrificing goals	Goals of *enlightened self-interest*
Unrealistic goals	*Realistic* goals

All of the improper goals in the left-hand column stand in the way of our recovering our natural zest and motivation for living. Appropriate, reasonable, and clear goals increase the changes of a better life.

Written Statements of Goals

Depressed persons need to make a clear written statement of their goals, and they should expose these written goals to sympathetic critics for evaluation. Written statements of the main goals of our life help us to stop daydreaming about goals. They stop us from a life of aimless drifting, and they also stop us from going in a cycle of crises. Neither drifting nor bumping along are satisfying life-styles, and written goals force us to be specific and get down to serious business about where we want to go.

Here is a good example of Frank's set of written goals—

> I am a nineteen-year-old male high school graduate. I just barely made it through grade twelve because of too much social life and too little studying. I am not a serious person when it comes to school learning, but I am keen about auto mechanics and women. To live a satisfying life, I want:

1. Marriage, if at all possible, and one or two children.
2. I don't want to have my own business because the responsibility seems too heavy, but I do want to work as a mechanic in a good service station. I might have to change employers once or twice to find a good service station, but I want to be a good auto mechanic, working for a good boss.
3. I want a better-than-average income to spend on my family and my family's social life, and I could discipline myself to be reliable in my work as an auto mechanic in order to obtain this good income.

Here is Grace's written set of goals—

I'm a forty-four-year old, happily married woman whose youngest child is age eighteen and about to go to the university. My husband is a professional and loves his work. I am a part-time hairdresser. To live a satisfying life, I want:
1. My husband and I to retire early with income to travel.
2. Because my children have left home, I will need some business responsibility in the next ten years, until my retirement, in order to feel useful and to have responsibility. I will try to work full time as a hairdresser and will manage a beauty parlor if opportunity permits.
3. My hobby is photography, and I want to begin serious study and take some courses in this area.

Here is an example of Harry's written goals—

I am twenty-six, male, single, very poor employment record, require psychiatric medication to control my medical depressions and nervousness.

To live a satisfying life, I want:
1. To get in control of my moods and nervousness without medication if possible.
2. To live outside of institutions.
3. To have a wife, if possible, or if not possible, then at least two good friends.
4. To find a steady, simple laboring job.
5. To rent an apartment, own a car, and be able to pay all of my bills.

6. To grow old independently.

Test Your Goals to See If They Are Realistic

First, look at your personal resources. The nineteen-year-old did get through high school, which took some willpower—resource 1. He also knows he nearly failed, which took some insight—resource 2. He also has a specific ambition, which takes some self-knowledge—resource 3—and which shows clear motivation and interest—resource 4.

Second, look at your past performance. This nineteen-year-old has moderate accomplishments and no serious setbacks. He will have to do a little better to earn his mechanic's papers, but his expectations are reasonable, in light of his past performance. His danger is that he may still not settle down enough to be in a learning mood; but because he has such a specific interest in an area where there is large labor demand, his goals are realistic.

Third, look at your present situation. The forty-four-year-old woman saw no serious unresolvable conflicts between her present responsibilities (a little housework for her and her husband) and her employment goals. Were she to have three small children still at home, she would have to weigh the pros and cons of going to work outside the home.

Also, the twenty-six-year-old male admits it is pointless to aspire to be prime minister. He recognizes his present weaknesses of uneven mood and regular need for institutional care and decides that happiness, independent living, and a minimum of conveniences are high enough goals for him to aim toward at this time.

What Are Intermediate Steps?

They are short-term goals and intermediate goals that are merely forward steps on the way toward our major goals, and you must plan these steps. You don't plan goals; you set them. But you do plan the route, resources, and activities that can get you to the goal. This is what planning is all about. Planning bridges the gap between where we are now and where we want to be. Planning is foreseeing our desired objectives in terms of the many steps that will get us to these objectives. Planning is the drawing of the "blueprint" we expect to follow to get us to the goal. Planning involves scheduling our actions and plotting the best use of our time, money, and effort. Planning begins in our thoughts, as we think how to do it, and then leads to the best course of action to reach the goal.

Organizing: Reaching Goals with a System

As each of us struggles to get the best, we try and discard many unworkable systems. We may have tried many systems and then discarded them. We probably saw these systems working successfully for others and borrowed them wholesale, only to find out that a system that works well for one person may not work for someone else. The right system is often the way out of depression.

Relationship of Goals to Systems

Goal	System
To save $50.00 per month	Set up a separate savings account in another bank.
To meet new people	Join three or four clubs and social organizations.
To pass an exam	Attend classes and try to anticipate exam questions and prepare for these.
To lose weight	Try a fad diet.

Each of the above systems does work well for certain people but not for others. Successful people have found systems that work for them. The system may not be entirely rational or logical, but the system must fit the individual, suit his strengths and weaknesses, and work for him.

There are many systems or organized approaches to a problem that aim to help us break such bad habits as wasting time or overspending money or overeating. Part of organizing is finding the right system. Habits are usually hard to break, and systems can help us break the

Change Your Depressive Behavior

habit. They can also help us keep good habits. Ideally, a good system stays around long enough to become a good habit.

It is most important to look for good systems in the right places. If you want a good system for learning assertive behavior, read the books on assertiveness—don't ask aggressive alcoholics. If you want to learn to be emotive, don't ask an inhibited, upper-class Englishman; watch and copy an emotional East Londoner.

Designing a System to Reach Your Goals:

If we can't borrow a ready-made system like A.A. or Smith's assertive system or Bach's system for fighting fairly in marriage, then we have to design our own system. This involves the following:

1. *Set your goals clearly and explicitly.* Define any key terms carefully.

2. *Know your own weaknesses* and build your system to account for your weaknesses. For instance, if you work best in a tight system that won't let you procrastinate or sabotage yourself, then design your system to allow you little choice or freedom. But if you respond to a system that trusts you and allows you an open opportunity to respond to each new opportunity, then design a loose system of guidelines and keep to them.

3. *Do you need deadlines* to meet and schedules to follow? Then knowing this about yourself, set your deadlines and keep to them.

4. *Build rewards* for yourself into your system. This means that the system rewards you for following it.

5. Does the system have *an appropriate starting date?* Allow time to think the system through carefully but not to procrastinate.

6. *Ask for help.* Bankers can help with a system to get control of our spending. Clergymen, lawyers, child-care workers, psychologists—there are many who can help you become a better system builder.

The Keys of the Kingdom

The committed Christian has two depression-fighting, life-encompassing goals, and these two goals breed excitement, realistic optimism, and a sense of thrilling adventure.

The first goal is the formation of a meaningful personal relationship with God through Jesus Christ. This relationship begins with repentance (character change) and proceeds with faith (confidence), then adds hope (confidence in the future) and continues into active love for others and God. This goal involves a constructive, progressive, disciplined, unending relationship between the Christian and God. However, the relationship is partnership, and the Christian can become depressed if he senses he is not being honorable and fair in the partnership. When this occurs, the Christian must:

(1) rethink his goals,
(2) renew his commitment, and then
(3) take on some great projects for the Kingdom.

Notice the order of these three points. The great projects for the Kingdom must be step 3, or else depression could increase because the inner changes (steps 1 and 2) did not take place to prepare him for step 3. Steps 1 and 2 should involve talking to God and also talking in great detail and in strict confidence to several mature Christian friends. Remember, we always think better when we talk out loud.

The second goal is maximum participation in the work of the Kingdom through Christian congregations. The keys of the Kingdom were given by Jesus to each and every New Testament congregation, and in sum the keys amount to the gospel message—"God so loved the world, that He gave His only begotten Son." Congregations have the Great Commission to preserve and extend the gospel in their own communities, in surrounding communities, and then on a worldwide scale. If you have been discouraged and depressed that your congregation is not working well or if you are not working well in your congregation, reread this chapter line by line with just this idea in mind as you read. Then make what changes you need to make in yourself, especially in your beliefs, attitudes, and priorities. Then make plans to revise your goals and rediscover enthusiasm by joining the greatest project on earth, namely, preserving and extending the gospel of God's sovereign grace and love to the ends of the earth through your participation in your local congregation.

9
Turn Anxiety into Motivation

Comparing Anxiety and Depression

Anxiety, like depression, is a combination or pattern of emotions. The difference is that *fear* is the strongest emotion in the anxiety pattern, whereas *sorrow* always predominates in depression.

Strength of Emotions in Anxiety and Depression Patterns

Anxiety	Strength of Emotion	Depression
Fear	Always strongest	*Sorrow*
Sorrow	Often second strongest	Anger
Guilt	Often third strongest	Fear
Anger	Often fourth strongest	Guilt

The proper function of fear is to motivate to action. Fear is a natural motivator. Activity and change are often the result of fear. Anxious people are fearful people, and their fear motivates them to hurry and to attempt to change self and/or their situation. They are busy making an effort to resolve the fear which is such a strong component part of their anxiety.

But notice that the second emotion in axiety is often sorrow. Sorrow causes us to slow down and think about the why of our personal losses and failures. Because fear and sorrow are opposites in the behavior which they prompt, the anxious person is full of inner conflict, with the fear speeding him up and the sorrow slowing him down. In the same moment the anxious person gets these two conflicting emotional messages, fear saying, "Go and do," and sorrow saying, "Stop, wait, and think." However, in anxiety the fear message is the stronger one.

Anxiety Can Change to Depression

In the anxious person fear motivates him to action. But if the action fails to bring satisfaction, the person classes himself as having failed, and this may add to sorrow. Each action which fails may increase sorrow to the point where it equals fear; then the person becomes equally anxious and depressed. If the sorrow increases further and exceeds the fear, then anxiety has changed to depression.

To illustrate how anxiety can change to depression, think of anxiety and depression as collections of test tubes, with the liquid level in each tube representing the strength of each emotion. The emotional pattern is called anxiety when the fear level is strongest, and the emotional pattern is called depression when the sorrow level is strongest. But they can be equal, in which case the person is as anxious as he is depressed. The patterns can also switch back and forth, so that a person is anxious one week, depressed the next week, and anxious again the week after that, and then equally anxious and depressed the next week. The following diagram illustrates how even a slight increase or decrease in the strength of the two emotions, sorrow and fear, can cause a basic change from anxiety to depression, or from depression to anxiety.

As an example of an anxiety pattern that switches to depression, a student is anxious about an upcoming exam, then takes and fails the exam and becomes depressed. Or a parent is anxious about a teenager's petty delinquencies, but when the teenager is sent to juvenile detention, the parent becomes depressed.

Comparing Anxiety and Fear

Anxiety often appears, on the surface, as if it were simply fear; and some people make the mistake of equating anxiety and fear. But anxiety is more complicated than *fear* and includes anguish and sor-

ANXIETY AND DEPRESSION PATTERNS

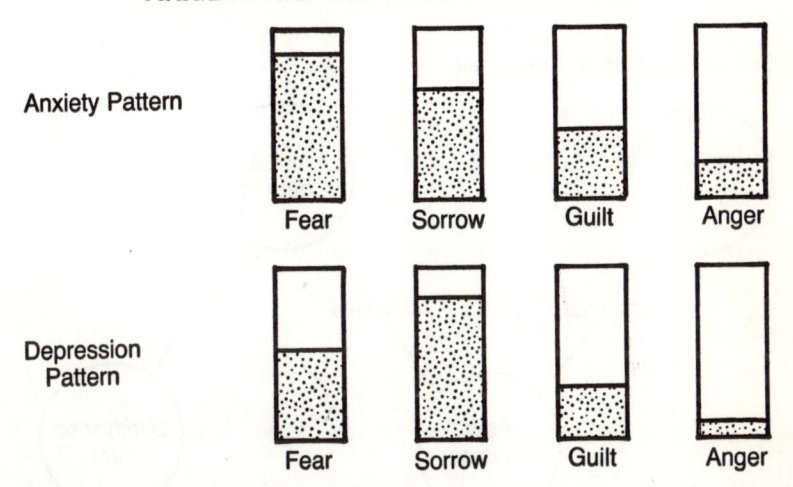

Anxiety Pattern

| Fear | Sorrow | Guilt | Anger |

Depression Pattern

| Fear | Sorrow | Guilt | Anger |

row over personal losses or failures, *guilt* (blaming self), and *anger* (at others and/or self). Suppose one person has a fear of illness, such as cancer. This fear may be due only to a chest pain, and after the person gets a good medical checkup and there are negative findings, the fear subsides. But in the next person the fear may be a long-standing fear because his mother died of lung cancer. The fear of cancer may then be associated with the fear of death, and this fear may be associated with unresolved sorrow and grief over the mother's death. The fear may also be associated with guilt over smoking two and a half packs of cigarettes daily, this guilt over smoking being due to one's belief that cigarettes cause cancer. Finally, the fear may be associated with anger at self for the lack of willpower to stop smoking. In the next diagram this example shows the usual complexity of anxiety.

We human beings are very complicated because of our powerful memories and our abilities to perceive the full complexity of life. Anxiety is the result of our complexity and is itself a complex emotional pattern dominated by fear. We must look for related sorrow and anguish over personal losses and failures. Finally, we must see if guilt and anger are also related to our dominant fears. If we analyze

COMPARISON OF FEAR AND ANXIETY

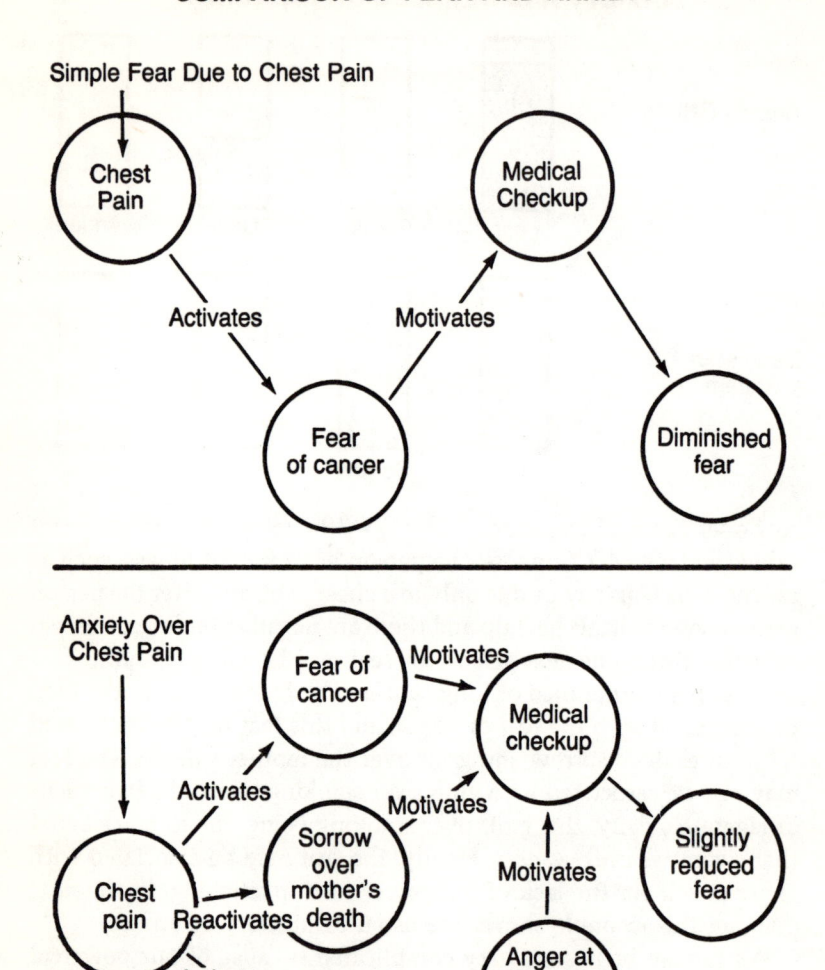

Simple Fear Due to Chest Pain

Chest Pain → (Activates) → Fear of cancer → (Motivates) → Medical Checkup → Diminished fear

---

Anxiety Over Chest Pain

Chest pain → (Activates) → Fear of cancer → (Motivates) → Medical checkup → Slightly reduced fear

Chest pain → (Reactivates) → Sorrow over mother's death → (Motivates) → Medical checkup

Chest pain → (Activates) → Guilt over smoking → (Activates) → Anger at self for lack of willpower → (Motivates) → Medical checkup our anxiety successfully, a pattern should emerge, which shows the anxiety to be much more complicated than the fear which triggers it.

Understanding Fear

Fear is the dominant emotion in anxiety. Fear includes mild apprehension but can range in strength all the way to panic, dread, and terror. The function of fear is to give danger signals to spur us to action. The signals are warnings that deadlines are approaching for the beginning of urgent courses of action. Fear warns us that we are running out of time to take action to avoid specific failures or to accomplish necessary successes. The fear is a direction finder, pointing us to a problem that needs our attention. Then it becomes an attention holder as we are urged to maintain the problem area in our consciousness until we resolve it.

Fear works in stages, and in the first stage it gives a burst of *mental energy* to assess the danger and plan how to deal with it. This extra mental energy keeps anxious people awake at night. It also makes them study for exams, finish work assignments, engage in many types of creative work, and plan escapes and avoidance.

After providing mental energy, *fear* then gives a burst of *muscle energy* to execute our plans. Fear is such a strong motivator that we sometimes act excessively in overacting, overtalking, overspending, working to exhaustion, or worrying about unlikely possibilities.

The basic fears include:

(1) fear of pain,

(2) fear of death,

(3) fear of loss of love and friendship. Many anxious spouses fear a marriage breakup. Many parents fear the departure of their sons and daughters from the family setting.

(4) fear of failure (marital, social, and/or financial),

(5) fear of loneliness,

(6) fear of loss of meaning and purpose.

Each of these fears is adaptive or life-preserving in itself; but if bad habits or unsound values are present, then the adaptiveness of these fears is canceled. An example is the woman who fears the breakup of her marriage, but is in the rut of passive resistance and also believes that it is too late to do anything to save the marriage. In this case her fear is initially adaptive, but her passivity and her futility later discount the usefulness of her fear.

Anxiety—a Natural and Normal Motivator

Anxiety, as the fear-dominated pattern of the negative emotions, is a *natural or normal motivator,* which challenges a person to react adaptively to the dangers, inconveniences, *and* opportunities of life. Anxiety is essential for survival, and the ideal is to have just the right amount of anxiety, and to regulate the anxiety to serve our own purposes. Anxiety must be reshaped, redirected, and strengthened or weakened as appropriate, so that it stays in line with our own best interests. It is only a problem in itself if it is misunderstood or ignored.

Anxiety spurs us onward toward *our own ideal of life.* This ideal is usually very different for each person, but the most common values in our ideal are:

Life itself—survival;

Health—spurring us toward proper diet, adequate exercise, and adequate rest;

Freedom and Security—spurring us toward personal, social, financial, and marital security;

Involvement and Status—spurring us toward satisfying intimate relationships, good friendships, and enjoyable employment;

Self-respect—spurring us toward a proper attitude to oneself and a balanced measure of self-love, self-acceptance, and self-confidence;

Meaning and Purpose—spurring us toward a philosophy of life that gives a sence of direction, usefulness, and structure to our daily activities.

Anxiety is spurring us to all of these good things. It *decreases* when we are making progress toward them, and it *increases* if these are endangered or lost.

Anxiety is not to be endured; *it is to be responded to.* The uneasiness, "butterflies" in the stomach, "being all choked up," sweating, heart pounding, pulsations, nausea, dizziness, and other discomforts of anxiety are intended to be unsettling and are supposed to shake us up and get us going to solve a problem. In most of us, this response of anxiety is moderate, balanced, and effective, and we need our anxieties in order to make the best of life.

Reason Makes Anxiety Effective!

The greatest advantage of anxiety in most people is that anxiety provides the motivation to struggle for a better life, but struggle or effort by itself rarely brings a better life. What is necessary is struggle or effort that is guided by sound reason. The sound reason guides our struggle onto the right track. Reason gives anxiety a winning combination, a successful strategy, and the energy to make it work. Reason makes anxiety effective.

Excessive and ineffective anxiety just go on making a person miserable. Such anxiety has no positive results, yet it is not the anxiety that is the problem. The problem is bad habits, false beliefs, and unsound values that render the anxiety ineffective. But just give a person with ineffective anxiety a new approach to his problem, and change his attitude and outlook by new habits and values that are based on sound reason. Suddenly the anxiety is helpful. That person begins to obtain more of what he wants from life, and the anxiety begins to regulate itself at a balanced, tolerable level. The key to anxiety regulation, then, is finding and accepting reasonable beliefs and values, which are fully discussed in an earlier chapter but should be reviewed again if necessary.

The Best Anxiety Reducers

There are both effective and ineffective anxiety reducers. The ineffective anxiety reducers reduce anxiety for a few minutes or hours, but then increase the anxiety higher than before. The following activities do in fact reduce anxiety, but only temporarily, so they are ineffective:
- eating
- smoking

- getting a headache (Believe it or not, headaches *reduce* anxiety!)
- daydreaming
- worrying
- using alcohol

All of these anxiety reducers should be avoided because they make matters worse minutes or hours later.

The best anxiety reducers are the following:

1. *Talking About Causes of Anxiety.*—We should talk and reason honestly and openly about what we think are the causes of our anxieties. This should lead us to take action to be that balanced person mentioned above, who has: proper diet, proper exercise, proper rest, good physical health, proper attitudes toward oneself, balanced feelings of self-love, self-trust, and self-acceptance, realistic personal goals and reasonable hopes for the future, satisfactory intimate relationships, good friendships, stimulating employment, emotional openness and emotional honesty, an assertive philosophy of life that encourages us not to hit back at others but not to back down either, and to stand up to others and insist on our fair share. Each of the points in this long list contributes its own ingredient to blend together a relaxed person whose anxieties are workable. If we are short on any of these points, there is no alternative but to get to work on them by talking toward a clear understanding and then taking action.

2. *Talking About Emotion.*—Anxiety is a combination of emotions including fear. Did you know that just the mere act of naming our emotions and describing them in detail in their physical form has an amazing calming effect! In fact, we can easily control the level of the anxiety by the amount we name and describe it to others around us: The more we express the anxiety, the lower it becomes. This is the golden key to anxiety reduction. Many people bore us with constant talk about their fears and tensions; but if they ever stopped talking and tried to hold it all in, they would soon experience disaster. To express anxiety is to reduce and control it.

3. *Moderate Exercise.*—Running, stretching, laughing, yawning, hugging, punching a punching bag, walking around the block, and physical work all tend to reduce anxiety effectively because we are taking action and using up the anxious energy.

Change Your Depressive Thinking

4. *Deep Breathing.*—Take two seconds to fill your lungs with a very deep and comfortable breath that pushes out your belly, then take fifteen seconds to let the breath out very slowly and evenly through your nose, so that a feather balanced on your upper lip would not blow away as you are exhaling. Anxiety is greatly reduced by repeating these deep breaths for a minute or two. Focus on exhaling slowly and evenly.

5. *Concentrating.*—Anxiety is reduced when we concentrate our attention on anything unrelated to our fears, such as a feather balanced on our upper lip, or our belly button, or on relaxing our right hand and arm, or on our shoes, or on a sound, or on a pleasant memory or a mathematical problem. Alpha waves in our brain are a sure sign that we are relaxing and becoming alert, and brain alpha waves increase if we take time to concentrate our attention—especially if we concentrate our attention on exhaling slowly and evenly or if we concentrate on relaxing our muscles. In the case of concentration, not only is anxiety reduced but muscle tension is reduced as well. Never try to blank your mind; instead, concentrate on something pleasant.

Control and Reduce Muscle Tension

1. All anxiety reducers help to *control* muscle tension, but other techniques *reduce* it.

2. *Deep muscle relaxation.*—When muscles remain tense from habit, we must retrain them to relax. The expression "deep" means that muscles stay tense in the core or center of the muscle. To relax the center of a muscle requires many *commands to relax,* not just one command. First, tense the bicep on your right arm. Second, study the feeling of tension. Third, relax, *studying the feeling of letting go.*

Then, when you think the muscle has let go completely, *tell it to let go even further.* Give the muscle time to relax, and *remind it again and again to relax even further.* This final stage of almost complete muscle relaxation is called deep muscle relaxation or progressive relaxation. It becomes easy only by much practice. Begin by relaxing your feet; then move up the legs and body to the arms and head relaxing every part.

3. *Exercise.*—Moderate exercise before relaxing helps muscles to relax further, but heavy exercise makes muscles stay tense. So do several easy knee bends, enjoy a walk up and down stairs twice, bend forward leisurely and touch your toes, and then sit down and practice relaxing.

4. *Stretch.*—A very effective relaxing technique is Hatha yoga, where the whole emphasis is on gently stretching the muscles. How do you get rid of muscle tension? You gently stretch it away. Use any exercise you wish for the muscles that are tense, and make the purpose of the exercise to be a stretch—a very gentle stretch. Especially for the back and neck, bend and pull and stretch the muscles in all directions very gently. Remember the old saying of India: To stay young forever, keep your spine flexible by bending and stretching. One excellent natural stretch that helps to eliminate anxiety and muscle tension is the yawn. Laughing is another natural stretch. Four good stretching exercises are: slow neck rolls and bends, gentle back bends and rolls, twisting at the waist, and standing and stretching one hand and arm above the head as high as possible.

5. *Massage.*—Muscles relax more quickly and more completely if they are pressed and squeezed gently. The pressure should come *gently* from the pads of the fingers, and the movement should be slow.

Massage your face and neck. Use gentle pressure on the forehead, around the eyes, cheeks, and mouth in order to pull and squeeze facial muscles.

6. *The One-Minute Plan.*—To reduce anxiety and relax muscles:

(1) Take five seconds and *sit down.*

(2) Take thirty seconds for one or two comfortable *deep-breathing* exercises.

(3) Take fifteen seconds to *concentrate* on relaxing your right hand and arm.

(4) Take ten seconds to *relax* your face, neck, shoulders, stomach, hands, arms, and legs. This sequel must be practiced many times, and as it becomes a habit, it will control most anxiety attacks.

7. *The Seven-Minute Plan*

(1) Lie down on your back and loosen clothing and get comfortable.

(2) Take two minutes for deep breathing.

(3) Take two minutes to gently exercise those muscles that are tense; tighten them slightly for ten seconds each, then let them relax; then relax them further and further.

(4) Take three minutes to lie motionless and concentrate on breathing deeply and exhaling through the nose so slowly that a feather on the upper lip would not move.

Summary

Anxiety is a pattern of emotions dominated by fear. Anxiety sometimes leads to depression if efforts to resolve it result in frequent failures.

Anxiety is more complicated than fear, and anxiety is best resolved by understanding its complexity, which includes sorrow, guilt, and anger.

Anxiety is a natural and normal motivator, which spurs us onward toward our basic life objectives. It is only a problem if it is not guided by sound reason.

The best anxiety reducers are: talking about the causes of anxiety, talking about our emotions, moderate exercise, deep breathing, and concentration.

Anxiety control is a facet of self-control which has been considered separately.

Anxiety in Christ

Christ brings peace of mind, unless we need anxiety to motivate us toward character change. But anxiety, even for motivation, can be excessive. To return excessive anxiety to constructive anxiety, examine the fear that is the core of your anxiety. Is the fear rational? It ought to be. Is the fear in proportion to the dangers in your life? It ought to be. Is the fear a habit response that originated in past dangers and is no longer adaptive for you at this time? It ought *not* to be.

Practice God's presence in order to bring your fears back to reality and proportion. God's presence is, after all, the main factor in assessing danger. "The Lord is near; have no anxiety, but in everything make your requests known to God in prayer and petition with thanksgiving. Then the peace of God, which is beyond our utmost understanding, will keep guard over your hearts and your thoughts, in Christ Jesus" (Phil. 4:7).

Yet, appropriate anxiety is often necessary. Paul sent a scolding letter to the church in Corinth "out of great distress and anxiety; how many tears I shed as I wrote it! But I never meant it to cause you pain; I wanted you rather to know the love, the more than ordinary love, that I have for you" (2 Cor. 2:4). So Paul knew severe anxiety, but he used it to perform a very difficult task that he knew he had to do. So should we capitalize on our anxiety, and go ahead and do what we ought to do, as difficult and as unpleasant as it may be.

Constructive anxiety results in positive action! Paul also said, "Apart from these external things, there is the responsibility that weighs on me every day, my anxious concern for all our congregations" (2 Cor. 11:28-29). What a positive force—constructive anxiety for Christ's congregations, which are the strategic work units of His Kingdom.

Part 4
Change Your Pattern of Emotional Expression

Part 4

10
Emotional Openness and Honesty

Mental health and regular honest expression of emotion go hand in hand. Emotions are for expressing, not suppressing. Positive and negative emotions are both healthy when they are honestly let out in the open.

An important step out of depression is learning new habits of regular, honest, emotional expression. If we have learned emotional deceit, we must discard it and overcome culture and family tradition to become emotionally honest. Continuous, accurate, emotional expression is a critical part of depression relief and is sometimes important in depression resolution as well.

This chapter identifies and condenses the salient points of all the current literature on the learning of emotional expressiveness, but most of the credit should go to the originating and scholarly work by Andrew Salter, entitled *Conditioned Reflex Therapy* (Capricorn Books, New York, 1949), which, in turn, was based on the work of Ivan Pavlov.

Emotional Habits

Habits are the basis of human behavior, and humans are creatures of extreme habit. We will usually go to any length to hang on to our old habits even if they make us unhappy!

The important habits of life are the ones that regulate expressions of our emotions. Behavior is only partly determined by intellectual reasoning or insight or knowledge—it is usually determined by habits, especially emotional habits.

The important thing about habits is that they are automatic reflexes. They cause us to act quickly and spontaneously *without thinking* in a way that is our customary behavior. That is why good habits make life easier and pleasant—they are there to be used without mental effort whenever we need them!
- Happiness is the habit of sharing our true feelings.
- Unhappiness is inhibition—the habit of hiding emotions.
- *Personal emotional growth is* always toward the breaking of unnecessary emotion *inhibitions* and the development of a sense of freedom and confidence in expressing one's true inner emotional self.

Inhibition Works By Stages

The inhibited person has as much *inner* feeling as the rest of us, but he hides, disguises, camouflages, and denies it. As this inner feeling boils inside and turns and twists, and as it tries to get out in the open but is stuffed back down inside, the emotional pressure builds up. As the inhibited person battles to contain this pressure, it requires his energy and concentration, at which point he appears outwardly to others to be:
- Unfeeling (even though he is stuffed with emotion),
- Uninterested in others (this is true, as interest is now directed desperately toward self-control),
- Placid and flat,
- Wrapped up in himself,
- Contented or indifferent.

However, this dishonest behavior leads the inhibited person to the next stage of even greater emotional pressure as he:
- Feigns contentment or indifference,
- Masks real feelings,
- Uses words that disguise the emotions and give a false impression,
- Never shouts or verbalizes honestly,
- Explodes at the breaking point and suffers from the explosion because it is now too strong to match the cause that triggered it.

As a result, there is no reduction of tension or inner emotional pres-

Change Your Pattern of Emotional Expression

sure, and cracks now appear in his emotional armor. The negative feelings begin to leak out, showing him to be in a moderate depression where he appears: Frustrated and confused, Discontented, Indecisive, Discouraged.

As the inner emotional pressure increases, the inhibitory person still feigns, masks, misleads, and disguises. His behavior shows him to be in a serious depression. The characteristics of this final stage of inhibition read like a textbook on depression: illogical thinking, lack of energy, extreme moodiness, loss of hope.

To illustrate these deepening stages of depression, the diagram on page 114 compares depression to the increasing pressure of a pressure cooker, while the depression resolution is the emotional expression of the escaping steam when the safety valve opens.

Many Faces of Inhibition

The inhibitory person can be described in many ways:

1. *He has a gambler's face,* completely concealing all personal feelings. This is a stone face, and the other players get no idea of what is really inside.

2. *He has constipation of the emotions,* needs to have emotional bowel movements, even needs emotional diarrhea, though not dysentery. This crude physical analogy is Salter's example and is included because it is so useful.

3. *He has a nauseated emotional stomach* and should vomit up the painful, nauseating emotion but instead tries to keep it down and digest it.

4. He is like a *chameleon,* who tries not to have its own color but disguises itself by taking on the emotion that is in its surroundings.

5. He is like *flypaper,* and every negative emotion sticks to him and he cannot shake it off.

6. He is like a kitchen *pressure cooker* that has the pressure release valve sealed shut, which means the emotional pressure builds up until there is a painful and destructive explosion.

Words and phrases that describe emotionally inhibited people: emotionally dishonest, impersonal, thinking and planning but not doing and not expressing, undemonstrative, polite, nice, formal,

HOW DOES INHIBITION LEAD TO DEPRESSION?
The Example of the Pressure Cooker

The Safety Valve
—putting our emotions into words and other forms of emotional expression

The Lid
—our habit of holding in our emotions

The Steam
—our unexpressed emotions

The Pressure Cooker
—our body and brain

The Heat
—all the irritations and frustrations of life

Stage 1: We are distressed or angry, and we politely pretend happiness instead of showing the distress and anger. This is *inhibition*.

Stage 2: We continue to feel the distress, and the pressure becomes a burdensome preoccupation which interferes with present pleasures.

Stage 3: The pressure increases, bringing with it indecision, discontent, and discouragement. Cracks appear in the emotional armor; outbursts, crying, and confusion appear.

Stage 4: Unexpressed emotions multiply the pressure, and there is illogical thinking, lack of energy, extreme moodiness, and loss of hope. This is *depression*.

masking, concealing, hiding, faking, feigning, disguising, distorting, twisting, camouflaging, a fraud, a hypocrite, secretive, apologetic, indecisive, moody.

Examples of Inhibited Talk:

1. How are you? Answer: "I'm fine, thank you, and how are you?"
2. How are you feeling today? Answer: "I don't know."
3. Would you like coffee or tea? Answer: "It doesn't matter—either would be fine."
4. Where would you like to spend our holidays this year? Answer: "Wherever you would like."
5. Is that a new dress? It looks beautiful. Answer: "Oh, no, it's just one of my old rags."
6. May I kiss you? Answer: "I guess, if you want to."
7. Something is bothering you. Answer: "Oh, it's nothing really."

What Are Emotive People Like?

Emotional openness and honesty is the basis of happiness and mental health. The emotive are beautiful people, and their beauty comes from good habits of expressing emotions regularly, accurately, honestly, openly, and quickly. Above all, the emotive are *genuine and transparent* about their emotions. They let it all hang out—almost.

If we pause to consider what we have done when we felt happiest, we recognize that we spoke without thinking and expressed our innermost feelings. This is what it means to be emotionally open and honest.

Other Characteristics of Emotive People

1. They are emotional, but they do not appear to be because their emotional pressure is usually low, and the feelings expressed are being felt *now*. They appear logical because they are thinking clearly and there are no old pent-up, unexpressed emotions to confuse them. They do not struggle to be logical; they struggle to be emotive.

2. They rarely explode emotionally, and they never lose control of their emotions. Why? They don't explode because they keep the

pressure down, and they never lose control because their control is from no control at all—just keeping the pressure very low.

3. To keep their thinking clear, they keep on emoting, so that they keep their mental machinery from getting gummed up with old emotions. Keep the wiring clean!

4. They enjoy responsibility, they are usually relaxed, and they are always frank. They are decisive and take immediate constructive action. They are energetic, but there is nothing hyperthyroid about them. They sincerely like people but are not seriously influenced by what others may think. They are never stuffed shirts. And they have all of these qualities because they do not need to consume any of their own strength to hold in their emotions.

5. Their emotional honesty is usually appreciated by others, who find them easy to trust, easy to like.

6. Inhibited people sometimes think they are superior to their emotive neighbors, but this is not true in any sense whatever. The emotive people have all the fun and are always the ones who get the job done with the least fuss.

7. It is quite a shock to our inhibited friends if we change our habits and become less inhibited ourselves. They may or may not like the change, but that is entirely up to them.

Learn All About Your Own Emotions

1. They are physical and are the pains and pleasures of our muscles and organs.

2. They occur simultaneously—that is, three or four different emotions can occur at once. Emotions share our moments on a percentage basis. Example—"In the same instant I am happy that today is payday, partly worried about being late for work, enjoying the song on the radio, tired, and aching in the neck and shoulders."

3. Some emotions—love, hate, and fear—are complex emotions, where our brain evaluates the potential pains or pleasures of a situation or person. These are adding-machine emotions where the brain adds up the pros and cons. While the emotion with the highest total fills our awareness, the other emotions are present but in the back-

Change Your Pattern of Emotional Expression

ground. It is most important to express complex emotions, or else we do not become aware of the emotions in the background.

4. Emotions accumulate and build up pressure in us as we experience them.

5. To express an emotion is to reduce it slightly.

6. Talking, touching, laughing, and crying are nature's ways of expressing emotion, but talking is the best way.

What You Feel Is What You Should Express

Consider the following questions often:

1. What do I love? Who do I love?
2. What do I hate? Who do I hate?
3. What do I hate in the persons I love?
4. What do I love in the persons I hate?
5. What do I fear? Who do I fear?
6. What do I fear in the persons I love?
7. What do I dislike in the persons I like?
8. Do I have ambivalence, where the love and hate are equal and cancel each other out and leave me feeling "numb" or indifferent or flat?
9. Am I afraid that certain things may happen?
10. Do I feel disgusted, proud, embarrassed, or ashamed of myself?
11. Do I feel tired, depressed, anxious, nervous, ambitious, lazy, enthusiastic, or discouraged?

From this list of questions, we should realize that it is a full-time job to express emotions. We need to work at it every day.

Talking Is Expressing

Man, the talking animal, has a marvelous way with words. But this talking animal is happiest when he shares honestly, in words, what he is really feeling. Talking about emotions is an excellent way to resolve depression. Be emotionally outspoken. Be a feeling talker, not a fact talker. Say "I," and then describe the feelings of the moment. When others respond to our feelings with "Why?" then do not react to their why, but simply return to an inward inspection of all your present emotions, and then describe each one in turn, beginning with the strongest. Here are some examples of emotive talk.

Remark	Type of Emotion
I like soup.	Liking
I detest that man and everything he stands for.	Disliking
That shade of green is perfect for you.	Praise
Thank heavens, it's Friday.	Relief
Excuse me, but I was here first.	Complaint
I'll wait, even if it kills me.	Determination
My feet hurt.	Discomfort
Darling, I love you with all my heart.	Love
Now, that was stupid of me!	Self-criticism
There's nothing to it. I'll take care of it.	Confidence
Good grief, I feel terrible about it.	Anguish
I feel both good and bad toward her; good because . . . and bad because	Ambivalence
I'm afraid of what might happen.	Fear

Faces Talk Too!

We do not usually need to snarl like a tiger to express our emotions or grin like a Cheshire cat that has read Dale Carnegie, but we should match our face with our mood.

Tell it like it is—with eyes and eyebrows, with mouth and lips.

Many times a picture is worth a thousand words, and facial talk can be the fastest, most effective means of expressing what we feel.

If you feel it, wear it on your face. If you feel it, look it. Characteristics of faces that talk: smiles, tears, blushing, grinning, wincing, winking, frowning, closing eyes, wearing a long face, looking disgusted. Do not wear the gambler's mask!

Self-Love, Self-Trust, Self-Acceptance

Before trying to improve all the relationships in your life, first allow the right emotions toward your own self. These include:

1. *Self-love,* because the richness of my life comes mainly from being on good terms with myself. (Self-love is healthy, vital, and whole-

some, and is only selfish in an acceptable positive use of the word selfish). Because I relish being my own primary source of nourishment, I look to others only secondarily to supply emotional needs. Because I do exist only as a separate individual, all my relationships require me to be strong in myself in order to relate effectively to others.

2. *Self-trust,* because I realize my emotions are very reliable guides, and my life prospers when I trust my own feelings and listen to them.

3. *Self-acceptance,* because I have fears and weaknesses that are a real part of me, and admitting these fears and weaknesses to myself is a basis for my future personal emotional growth.

Expressing Anger in Intimate Relationships

Close or intimate relationships are the bread of life, and they begin on the basis of mutual ability to express love and concern. But mutual love and concern cannot make intimate relationships last and endure. The lasting intimate relationships are based on the mutual ability to show negative emotions, expecially anger.

So name your negative emotions and describe them often, but don't blame the other person for being the way he/she is. Listen to his/her anger, and try to understand that anger. It is anger without blame that heals. "I am honestly not blaming you for it, honey, but that is what I'm feeling now."

You Can't Hurt the Feelings of Others

Never worry that your emotional honesty may hurt the feelings of others, because they can only cause their own feelings to hurt and only you can cause your feelings to hurt.

This means that each person is responsible only for his own emotions and feelings and mood.

Our emotions are always a matter of choice, which we decide for the effect we want them to have on others, *or,* which we decide for our own enjoyment (as in the case of self-pity and most depressions), *or,* for a mixture of both reasons.

The Buildup of Sorrow and Anguish

The dominant emotion in depression is sorrow (remember that sorrow is the short form of a complex of traits, and the full form is sorrow-anguish-distress). If you feel sorrow, anguish, or distress, put it into words to friends and acquaintances. Let this emotional talk siphon off some of the sorrow and reduce the inner pressure. You will still have to work the sorrow through properly, but at least the sorrow will be kept at a less painful level for you. This lower level will help you to think straight when you start to work the sorrow through.

Sorrow, in the final analysis, is resolved only by accepting our losses and making required changes in our character and situation. But expressing sorrow certainly relieves sorrow temporarily, so that we can think about it effectively.

The Christian Quandary

"Have done with spite and passion, all angry shouting and cursing, and bad feeling of every kind" (Eph. 4:31).

There is no contradiction between the Christian ideal of perfect love for others and emotional expressions of firmness, toughness, discipline, and punishment. Firmness and toughness are often required in a Christian's response to others. Tough love is often necessary and can be consistently and wholesomely Christian when it is applied correctly. Discipline and punishment, when appropriate, are God-given motivators to personal growth and reformation. What are some interpersonal situations where perfect love calls for emotional expressions of firmness, toughness, discipline, punishment, or severity?

Unsatisfactory Situation	*Response of Christian Love*
Money changers and merchants move their business into the Temple.	Jesus evicts the money changers with physical force and deep feeling.
Two groups of hypocrites come for baptism only because of the social advantages.	John the Baptist calls a spade a spade, "[You poisonous snakes! Either change your *hearts* or forget

Change Your Pattern of Emotional Expression

	about the *outward act*]" (Matt. 3:7-8, author's paraphrase).
A hostess is so involved with her preparations that she ignores her guests.	Jesus talked directly and critically to her, though she was a true friend, "Martha, Martha, you are fretting and fussing about so many things [and neglecting what is most important of all. Rearrange your priorities]" (Luke 10:42).
A religious leader who is greedy and wicked takes offense at Jesus' table etiquette.	Jesus upbraided him, "You fool. [You fuss about trivial matters, and you] have no care for justice and the love of God" (Luke 11:40-42, author's paraphrase).
The president of the synagogue is furious that Jesus has healed a cripple on the sabbath.	Jesus answered, "What hypocrites you are! [Rejoice that she has been freed from her bonds!]" (Luke 13:15-16).
Peter shows lack of moral principles by refusing to eat his meals with non-Jews.	Paul confronted him directly in a church meeting with strong words and deep feeling.

Should Christians bottle up their frustrations, or should they express themselves regularly? They should express themselves, and if others are trying to find offense, deal with the matter directly and fairly. You may certainly be *firm* (saying *no* is often a loving response, even if others prefer *yes*) and *tough* (calling a spade a spade is plain honesty, and if truth is what is upsetting others, it is the time for them to be upset). To be firm in a loving way is to say no with the intention of helping the other person. To be tough in a loving way is to be truthful with the intention of helping.

Should Christians always be "nice"? No, if nice means sacrificing principle. No, if nice means avoiding problems that need to be faced. No, if nice means dishonesty. No, if nice means avoiding a constructive confrontation.

When nice means kindness and gentleness, and kindness and gentleness are appropriate, then and only then, "nice" is right.

11
Assertiveness

Are You Assertive in These Situations?

Do you speak up when someone breaks into a line ahead of you, or do you silently burn in anger toward that person? What do you do when you are being ignored by a salesclerk? You should speak up and interrupt the clerk's conversation with another clerk and ask for service. Can you say no when a salesperson has you pinned against the wall? Can you try on several suits in a clothing store and then buy nothing?

Can you:

	YES	NO
—ask for a date?	——	——
—walk into a meeting late?	——	——
—admit a mistake?	——	——
—ask a big favor?	——	——
—say no to sex?	——	——
—say no to alcohol?	——	——
—demand information from a doctor?	——	——
—go back to the cashier for the right change?	——	——
—be the one dissenting voice in your peer group?	——	——
—begin a conversation?	——	——

What is your score out of ten as you check off these situations? Are you an *assertive* person? Or are you *passive* or *aggressive?* This chapter

The Three Ways of Handling Conflict

Aggressive	Assertive	Passive
fight	talk	flight
push	stand my ground	back down
overwhelm	persist	give up
standing up for my own rights without concern for the rights of others.	standing up for my own rights without putting others on the defensive and while considering the rights of others.	not standing up for my own rights
wanting a settlement involving more than a fair share of benefits	wanting a settlement of the conflict that is fair, meaning a fifty-fifty equal sharing of the benefits and responsibilities of the relationship	accepting a settlement less than a fair share of benefits and responsibilities
coming to a settlement by threatening, badgering, harassing, verbal abuse, and a dominating attitude	coming to a settlement by talking, bargaining, trade-offs, compromise, and negotiating.	coming to a settlement by silence, giving in, backing down and avoiding
saying no with a vengeance	saying no without feeling guilty	saying yes when we want to say no, or saying no and feeling guilty

studies these three types of behavior, which are introduced by the diagram on page 124, The Three Ways of Handling Conflict. Study the diagram to see where your behavior fits.

Definition of "Assertiveness"

To assert: to insist on one's rights; to demand one's fair share, and fair means fifty-fifty or equal; to stand up to people when we are dissatisfied with a relationship or arrangement.

Assertive behavior is for conflict situations. Conflicts come when people disagree on how to distribute the benefits and responsibilities of their relationship. When there are no conflicts, then a certain amount of both aggressive and passive behavior is acceptable and, at times, even desirable. But conflict requires assertive behavior most of the time. Only when we believe the other person to be incapable of fairness or understanding should we use aggression or passivity in conflict situations.

The assertive person begins by stating his own view of what would be a more equitable distribution of the responsibilities and benefits of the relationship. If his view is then disputed, he expects to negotiate, to bargain, to compromise, to deal, to give and take, to arrange trade-offs, and even to haggle—all in the spirit of a desire for a mutually satisfying agreement.

An assertive act leads to a settlement—to a no-conflict situation, to a resolution. There are no losers on either side after an assertive settlement, and assertive people actually want the other side to win, too.

Assertive behavior omits blame. Blame and faultfinding are aggressive acts which focus on the past, while the real issue is not the past but the changes we want *now* (the present) in the relationship. Blame and faultfinding put us on the defensive; and then the fight is on and one side loses. Both fighting and blaming are aggressive acts, but asserting and compromising are what is needed.

Emoting usually precedes asserting. Emoting means expressing one's real feelings. Anger often needs to be expressed before assertive work begins. Asserting means stating one's view of a good settlement and defending it without fighting. Usually we have to emote first, which results in calming us down, after which we are calm enough to assert ourselves well.

No—the most beautiful word in the world. We must learn to say no to the demands that others make upon us. Everyone has the right to say no without feeling guilty. Don't blame others for the demands they make on you—decide if you want to go along with their demands, and if you don't, simply say no, and leave it at that.

Be Assertive at Home

Be assertive with your spouse, children, relatives, employer, and friends. In other words, be assertive with all those who are important to you. The basis of all close relationships is mutual agreement as to our responsibilities to each other. How satisfying these close relationships are depends on our assertiveness as we work out the details of the agreement. If we are aggressive in working out the agreement, we will get more than our fair share, and the other person will be unhappy and the relationship will suffer. If we are passive in working out the agreement, we will get less than our fair share, and then we will be unhappy ourselves and the relationship will suffer. Being assertive is being in the middle between aggression and passivity. We stand up for our own rights, but we give thought to the rights of others also. We want the agreement to be good for the other person, so he will go on keeping the agreement.

When we are assertive for the first few times, others are usually shocked at the change we have made. We need to be prepared for the shock of others, and we are wise to assure them that we want changes based only on mutual agreement, that we will only insist on what we think is our fair share, and that this is open to negotiation. They will wonder if the assertive change in us is permanent and will accept the change only as we persist in being assertive. They will wonder how much further we are going to change, and again we need to assure them that our plans are only to insist on the full share of our rights and to insist in a kind and reasonable, though firm, manner.

Assertiveness Is a Whole New Way of Living

To become assertive is to change our basic style of living. It is a big change, and it produces quite a reaction. As we use the assertive approach, we should proceed on a small scale at first and give ourselves time to practice and perfect it. We should expect that our first assertive attempts will be unclear and will give a mixed and confusing message; others may not really understand what we want and may resent our fumbling efforts. If they are irritated with us, we should understand this. But we must persist with our assertive behavior even if it is imperfect. We cannot give in or back down at this stage. We must insist on changes that we think will put the relationship on a fair footing; and others will soon grow to accept our insistence on our rights. Eventually they respect us for it.

Our Assertive Rights

The proponents of assertive skills, including Salter (1949), Bach (1968), Alberti (1970), and Smith (1975), all agree that each human being has basic rights that should govern interpersonal relationships. Here is a list of rights as set forth in the book *When I Say No, I Feel Guilty* (Manuel J. Smith, 1975, Dial):

1. You are the only one who has the right to judge your own behavior and take the responsibility for it. Some others—your spouse, parents, children, employer, banker, friends, clergyman—may think they have the right to judge you, but they don't.

2. You don't have to offer reasons and excuses for your behavior. Whenever others demand to know why you are doing something, it's a good time to tell them to back off and give you more breathing space.

3. Only you can decide how much you want to help others. You owe no help to others—you have no debt to repay. Help them only if you decide that is what you want to do. And if anyone says you owe him some help, set the record straight.

4. You have the right to change your mind. Don't let others guilt trip you into sticking with what you said last week or last year.

Change your mind, change your values, and change your life to become the kind of person you want to be.

5. You have the right to make mistakes and be responsible for them. Mistakes in life are commonplace, and they are usually not serious. Make your mistakes and learn your lesson for next time. If others have slipped into the habit of reminding you of your mistakes, then you remind them to cease and desist.

6. You have the right to say, "I don't know." Say it as often as necessary. You have the right because you are human, you don't have to know everything, and you don't have to be perfect.

7. You have the right to be independent of the goodwill of others before coping with them. This important right says, "Quit worrying about whether people will like you if you stand up for your rights. Stand up for your rights and let your friendships and love life get straightened around later."

8. You have the right to be illogical in making decisions. Emotions are often just as important as logic, and expressed emotions prepare us for good decisions, even if these decisions may appear illogical to others.

9. You have the right to say, "I don't understand." Others may think their explanations are always perfect the first time, but that's not true. You can ask them to repeat themselves over and over until you feel you understand.

10. You have the right to say, "I don't care." Others like to hold us to our former loyalties and loves. Though we may shock them, we have to say, "I'm sorry, but in all honesty I have to tell you that I no longer care about you (or that other person, or that organization)." Say it and be delivered from that old burden.

Assertive Talk Resolves Depressions

Many depressions are caused mainly by a passive attitude in marriage, parenting, or other interpersonal relationships. In such circumstances assertive behavior is the only solution. But how do you become assertive with someone you have known for years, especially a spouse or sons and daughters?

1. Have a talk with the person and tell him/her/them that you are going to start standing up for yourself more, and that in fairness (this is what assertiveness is all about) to them, you are telling them in advance.

2. Don't ask their permission or their opinion, because this would be passive; just tell them directly that you have decided to become a more assertive person.

3. Make your first assertive demand, starting with a small but meaningful demand. Expect to have to haggle and barter and negotiate in order to get what you want. Think in terms of trade-offs, but always start by asking for more than you want, and offering less than you are prepared to give in return. Then as the negotiating continues, you can make the terms easier on the other person and still get a deal that you think is fair to you.

4. Don't be in a hurry to complete an assertive arrangement. Usually others need time to think over the terms you have offered them, so expect that the arrangement may not be completed for days. But set a definite time for settling the matter, so that it doesn't drag on.

5. Don't listen too seriously to the demands of others; naturally they are standing up for themselves, too, and they want the best deal they can get. When they repeat their demands over and over, you do the same. Persistence is the first step of assertiveness, and simple repetition of our demands is what persistence is all about. Simply keep on saying in a calm voice what it is that you want.

6. As aggressive people feel the pressure of our assertive approach, they respond by threatening and accusing. "You don't love me anymore or you wouldn't do this to me." "If you do this, I'm leaving." We must ignore the threats and the accusations and let them do what they feel they must do unless it is at our expense.

7. "You are not being fair" is a common accusation, and when your spouse and children blame you for this they are partly right. Why? Because you taught them all these years that you were prepared to do a larger share, and now they believe that larger share is properly yours. So expect to be told that you are unfair. When this happens, answer, "I can understand why you feel that way when for years I was doing part of your share, but I did it voluntarily and I don't wish

to do it anymore. I'm sure you will be able to get used to this new way of everyone doing his own fair share." Then do only your fair share from then on.

Nellie McClung, a very assertive woman, said many years ago, "Never retreat, never explain, never apologize—get the job done, and let them howl." Sometimes, with our own families, it has to be this way for a while until they get used to our new assertive way of living. Don't be surprised if your new assertiveness makes them depressed just as it clears up your depression! Why do they get depressed? They soon realize that they can no longer have an easy time at your expense, and they are very unhappy at losing this advantage. But their depression is their problem—to be resolved by constructive character change in themselves.

Summary

Conflicts in relationships are best resolved by assertiveness, which is a persistent demand for a fair deal and an insistence on one's right to set the terms of one's own life. We must all have the strength to say no to the unfair demands of others. Depression is often caused by a passive attitude that lets others set the terms for us.

It's never too late to start to be assertive, especially in middle age and old age. Think it through, and begin.

Conclusions
Resolve Depression by Character Change

Conclusions

Depression is an unpleasant but necessary stage in personal growth and development. Depression is not mysterious and unexplainable; rather, it is rational, adaptive, and directly related to our personal problems. For this reason depression can be resolved, first, by understanding it, second, by getting the right attitude toward depression, third, by breaking bad habits that cause depression, fourth, by changing false beliefs that cause it, and fifth, by learning new personal and social skills that can lead out of depression. These five points are what this book is all about.

The Psychological Depressions

A very small percentage of depressions are biochemical, and for these this book is only a secondary help; the primary help for biochemical depressions is medical and psychiatric.

The large majority of depressions are psychological and characterological. A psychological depression is not a medical-psychiatric illness; neither is it the blue Mondays and brief blahs. Psychological depression is a mood crisis between these extremes and is a reaction to major loss or failure or disappointment. It is not crippling or paralyzing or hopeless and is intended, by the mind of the depressed person, to be a form of self-help. The outcome of depression should always be positive, as the depression accomplishes its purpose of removing barriers and encouraging subsequent personal growth. Psychological depression is usually a natural, adaptive, positive process intended to slow us down for a better look at ourselves, with a view to make significant personal changes and readjustments. It is intended to be a prod or normal motivator to engage in serious self-analysis and personal problem solving.

Depression Self-Analysis

Depression is a combination of at least four negative emotions:
1. Sorrow—the major depressive emotion
2. Anger
3. Fear
4. Guilt.

Depression self-analysis consists of analyzing the varying amounts of each of these four emotions as they occur, as well as asking why each is occurring, and deciding what should be done about each emotion. You have completed your depression self-analysis when you have ranked, in order of their strength, each of these four negative emotions as they occur in you, and when you have decided what steps to take to make the personal changes in your character and life situation that your depression requires.

Depression as Adaptive

Adaptive means having a useful purpose that adds to the quality of life. Adaptive responses are life-serving and useful. Depression is always intended by the mind to be adaptive for us, but we can lose this opportunity to adapt if we refuse to consider personal change and personal growth.

Depression is supposed to:
1. *Slow us down* for careful self-analysis.
2. *Focus our attention* on major problems for problem solving.
3. *Motivate* toward specific changes in us.
4. *Cushion* temporarily from intense psychological pain.
5. *Protect us* from rash decisions and the errors of haste.

Depression is a necessary and positive response of the negative emotions. It points us to critical areas of our life that are in need of repair and improvement and insists that we use our mental energy and ability to find solutions and put these solutions into adaptive changes that will satisfy us. Obviously, we shouldn't fight our depression, as it is not the problem. We should work through our depression successfully by making personal changes we need to make.

Adaptive Emotions

Not only is depression adaptive or life-serving, but each of the negative emotions of depression is also adaptive. Recall their adaptive features:

1. *Sorrow*—the major depressive emotion includes sadness, dejection, sorrow, and gloom. It contributes the slowing down and focusing features of depression, as it causes us to focus on major losses such as loss of spouse, loss of self-respect, or loss of health.

2. *Anger* is adaptive when expressed. It is the complaint emotion. Inner-directed anger is adaptive because it motivates to self-growth as we focus on our own inferiorities such as poor concentration, obesity, shyness, lack of willpower. Outer-directed anger is adaptive as it motivates us in the search for justice because of unfairness of family, friends, or organizations. Unexpressed anger increases depression, but anger expressed without blaming is a major source of depression resolution.

3. *Fears* are, of course, adaptive because they provide danger signals, plus mental energy to seek a solution to the danger, and then muscle energy to put the solution into effect. Fears also motivate us to predict and avoid future losses and failures.

4. The adaptive function of *guilt* is threefold:
   (1) It focuses on our ideals and gets us to aim at the maximum that is possible for us, not the minimum required for survival.
   (2) It gives us an aversion for lower standards and values.
   (3) It gives us an aversion for people who espouse lower standards and values.

From guilt we also get willpower, resistance to temptation, self-discipline and self-control; these are such valuable personal traits that guilt comes close to winning first prize for being the most adaptive of the negative emotions.

Goals and Enthusiasm

Depression gets us to think over the meaning and purpose of our life in order to improve it. It does this by motivating us to evaluate all possible alternative strategies to reach our goals. It also gets us to reevaluate our goals.

We should have written statements of our goals, and we should expose these statements to friends in order to get constructive criticism. We should test our goals to see that they are realistic. We should design a good system to reach our goals.

Writing an autobiography of the important influences of our life is good preparation for goal reevaluation.

Thinking and Reasoning Clearly

Clear thinking leads out of depression. Some depressions are due primarily to faulty thinking and reasoning. How do you rate yourself as a thinker? How do others rate you in terms of solving the often complicated problems of life? If you need to sharpen your thinking, try the following:

1. Allow yourself time to think. Don't be pressured for quick decisions.

2. Express your emotions *before* you settle down to think, and then emotions will have only a balanced part of your decisions.

3. Make sure your evidence proves your point. Does your conclusion logically follow from your facts?

4. Work hard at gathering the evidence.

5. Question yourself to see if your reasoning is based on facts, not prejudices.

True Beliefs and Sound Values

False beliefs and wrong values are major causes of depression. Studying our basic beliefs and values is useful because they are then confirmed as adequate or they must be replaced. Here is a short list of the most common true beliefs and sound values that lead out of depression:

1. *A is A.* Reality is reality, and it is never very hard to figure out if we use our own minds and ignore the mental games and dishonest secret strategies of others to control us and use us unfairly. Relationships are what they appear to us to be, not what others are faking and pretending them to be. Call a spade a spade, to the point of brutal honesty; trust your own mind and come to your own conclusions.

2. *Self-interest is often good and necessary.* Depression often means we have lost a noble and honorable sense of self. This noble sense means that my main responsibility is to make my life conform to the image of my highest ideals. This is the positive view of selfishness, which says I cannot and must not be secondary in any relationship; I must make each relationship be secondary to my life and my ideals.

3. *I am fully responsible for my life.* No one else is responsible for me. The world owes me nothing, not even a helping hand. My brother is not my keeper. My life is entirely up to me. I have to make my life work well. It is not up to anyone else.

4. *Everything has a rational explanation.* Myth, magic, mysticism—none of these can explain life and all of its complexities. Only reason can explain, by analyzing causes, what is the meaning and importance of experiences and events. Whatever problems and opportunities exist, only reason can help us make the best out of what we have.

5. *I am alone.* It is a mistake to overrate the importance of others, and mental health comes primarily from being on very good terms with self.

6. Other common *false beliefs that lead into depression:*
   (a) Individuals exist for the group.
   (b) I must always take others seriously.
   (c) I have no personal value.
   (d) I must depend on others.
   (e) Failures, mistakes, and the past are extremely important.

Emotional Openness and Honesty

Mental health and regular honest expressions of emotion go hand in hand. Emotions are for expressing, not suppressing. Positive and negative emotions are both healthy when they are honestly let out in the open.

One of the first steps out of depression is learning new habits of emotional expression. If we have learned emotional deceit we must discard it and overcome culture and family tradition to become emotionally honest.

To be genuine and transparent about our emotions takes courage because our inhibited friends would prefer that we stay the way we were. But it is always worthwhile to work to gain the valuable habits of expressing emotions regularly, accurately, honestly, openly, quickly.

The upper-class English were terribly wrong when they saw the proper civilized mature human adult as one who controls, dignifies, and camouflages emotion so that others do not know how he really feels. The lower-class Cockney East Londoners were right when they showed emotion quickly and honestly.

Anger is an especially healthy emotion when it is expressed. Anger at self is good, if appropriate, because it motivates to self-growth. Anger at others is good, if appropriate, because we then make our complaints in a search for justice. Honest anger restores love in intimate relationships, but it is anger *without blame* that is most helpful.

Assertiveness

To be assertive is to stand up to people and to insist on our rights without putting others on the defensive. Assertive behavior is for conflict situations, when people disagree on how to distribute the benefits and responsibilities of their relationships. The assertive person begins by stating his view of what would be a more equitable distribution of the benefits and responsibilities. Then, if his view is disputed by the other person, he expects to negotiate, to deal, to bargain, to compromise, to arrange trade-offs, and even to haggle, in order to get a mutually satisfying *agreement*. This agreement is the *goal*

Resolve Depression by Character Change

of assertive behavior to a no-conflict situation. There are no losers in an assertive settlement, and assertive people always want the other side to win, too. Assertive talk resolves many depressions.

Anxiety and Relaxation

Anxiety is supposed to be our great motivator to become a successful, balanced person. Anxiety and depression can work well together in pressuring us to break bad habits, to restructure relationships, and to set new goals for ourselves.

The goal of anxiety is to establish the following adaptive responses to life:

1. Proper diet
2. Adequate exercise
3. Adequate rest
4. Good attitude to oneself
5. Balanced measure of self-love, self-trust, self-acceptance
6. Good friendships
7. Satisfying intimate relationships
8. Enjoyable and secure employment
9. An assertive philosophy of life that does not hit back, but does not back down.
10. Emotional openness and emotional honesty.

When we are short of any of these adaptive responses, anxiety is supposed to spur us toward them. Anxiety is a complex emotional response intended to spur us to action.

Self-Control

Self-control includes willpower, self-discipline, and resistance to temptation. Lack of self-control is a major cause of depression. An adaptive goal of many depressions is the building and strengthening of self-control.

Do you have impulses, urges, and bad habits that are running your life and making you depressed?

The formula for greater self-control is:
- *Commitment,* in which we put self-control at the top of our list or

priorities, and we make it a battle to the finish to change in the direction of greater self-control.

• *Awareness,* in which we carefully analyze and study the part of our life we want to change. We itemize all component parts and note the relationship of the parts. We become an expert on the part of our character that we want to change.

• *Strategy,* in which we come up with a clever and practical plan to carry us through the stages of hard work that will result in inner personal change.

Self-Esteem

Character is the beliefs, values, and habits we have chosen to be ourself. Self-esteem and depression are opposite views of character. *Self-esteem* is liking our character, while *depression* is a complicated dissatisfaction with character. Depression ought to lead to character change, and the right kinds of character change lead to self-esteem.

Depression ⟶ Character Change ⟶ Self-Esteem

But character change is hard work. Our old habits hinder change. Our old friends want us to stay the same. Our own uncertainty also stands in the way, because we cannot know for sure if our efforts to change will succeed.

Shyness is a special problem in which we overvalue the opinions of others and we constantly seek their approval. The way out of shyness is a major series of successes and a conscious devaluing of the opinions of others.

The Christian View of Depression

The Christian understands that God's purpose is to bring something good out of every depression. In the Scriptures those who were depressed came through the depression as better persons, wiser persons, and persons who found more satisfaction in walking in God's way.

Christian prayer focuses on finding ways to come through depression successfully. The Christian accepts depression as a divine prod

Resolve Depression by Character Change

to work toward increased personal maturity, and this attitude leads to the prayer, "Lord, help me to work through my depression. Help me to outgrow my depression. Help me to change what I need to change in my life so that I can mature beyond depression."

God gets a perfect score for the design of all His creative work, especially His creation of man's mind. God made no mistake when He made us capable of depression, which is intended to be a painful but necessary first step toward personal change and growth. God can use depression to get us to focus on self-growth and self-improvement whenever it is necessary. Only if we refuse to focus on and achieve needed change—either characterological or situational change or both—do we get depressed.

The Christian philosophy is, "I must accept God, and I must walk in His ways. I must accept reality and change it where necessary. I must accept responsibility for my life, including my depression."

The world certainly needs more straight-thinking Christians. Straight thinking leads away from depression. Christians are the salt of the earth when they think straight, but they often fall into depression when they are muddleheaded. Congregations need to be straight thinking, too, if they are going to build Christ's kingdom effectively.

Depression is intended to result in character and situation change. This is the message of Scripture, and this is the message of science. God wants you to do better, and your depression is intended as a first step to a better life ahead. Can you understand this constructive and purposeful view of depression? Can you start to grow and mature beyond your depression? *Tuum est*—"It is entirely up to you." Jesus said, "I have come that men may have life, and may have it in all its fullness" (John 10:10). Slow down, think straight, and make some constructive changes in your life! That is the message of depression. Accept the message.